Routledge Revivals

Foundations of Faith Volume 4

Originally published in 1927, this is the final of four volumes to discuss Christian Theology, under the guidance of the historic decisions of the Christian Church and the prevailing tendencies of Catholic thought in the early 20th Century. This volume is concerned with subjects that can generally be summed up under the title Eschatology: that part of theology concerned with death, judgements and the final destiny of the soul.

Foundations of Faith Volume 4
Eschatological

W.E. Orchard

First published in 1927 by George Allen & Unwin Ltd.

This edition first published in 2024 by Routledge
4 Park Square, Milton Park, Abingdon, Oxon, OX14 4RN
and by Routledge
605 Third Avenue, New York, NY 10158.

Routledge is an imprint of the Taylor & Francis Group, an informa business

© 1927 W.E. Orchard.

The right of W.E. Orchard to be identified as the author of this work has been asserted by him in accordance with sections 77 and 78 of the Copyright, Designs and Patents Act 1988.

All rights reserved. No part of this book may be reprinted or reproduced or utilised in any form or by any electronic, mechanical, or other means, now known or hereafter invented, including photocopying and recording, or in any information storage or retrieval system, without permission in writing from the publishers.

ISBN 13: 978-1-032-89999-2 (hbk)
ISBN 13: 978-1-003-54570-5 (ebk)
ISBN 13: 978-1-032-90038-4 (pbk)
Book DOI 10.4324/9781003545705

FOUNDATIONS OF FAITH

IV

ESCHATOLOGICAL

BY THE
REV. W. E. ORCHARD, D.D

LONDON: GEORGE ALLEN & UNWIN LTD.
RUSKIN HOUSE, 40 MUSEUM STREET, W.C. 1

First published in 1927
(All rights reserved)

*Printed in Great Britain by
Unwin Brothers, Ltd., Woking*

FOREWORD

IN completing this Fourth Volume of expositions of the Catholic Faith, the magnitude and difficulty of the task have convinced the writer that this was something for which he possessed neither adequate knowledge nor ability; but it should be remembered that the whole work is not so ambitious as it appears, for it consists merely of collections of monthly Tracts which were published mainly in order to provide his congregation with some systematic doctrinal instruction that might form a background and supplement to ordinary preaching.

In the present volume the chapter on "Hell" has aroused controversy somewhat similar to that which was evoked by the chapter on "The Eucharist" in Volume III. Readers of the articles and comments that this has occasioned in some of our religious newspapers will perhaps be interested to see the full treatment of the subject, from which isolated statements have been selected as a basis for rigorous and sometimes quite uninformed condemnation. But it should be remembered that not only must the whole chapter on "Hell" be read, and all statements considered only in their context, but the chapters on the related subjects of "Judgment," "Purgatory," "Heaven" and "What determines Destiny?" must also be taken into account if a balanced judgment on this difficult and painful subject is to be attained.

FOUNDATIONS OF FAITH

Needless to say, however, the author claims no authority for merely personal opinions, but submits unreservedly and gladly to the teaching of the whole Church, whenever and wherever that is authoritatively declared.

The Author has to ask the indulgence of readers for the following corrections which need to be made in the text:

Page 13, line 21, read: *visible,* instead of, *invisible.*
Page 55, line 33, read: *an unquestionable,* instead of, *a unquestionably.*
Page 69, line 3, read: *hearts,* instead of, *heart.*

CONTENTS

	PAGE
FOREWORD	v
THE TWO WORLDS	1
BODY, SOUL AND SPIRIT	17
IMMORTALITY	33
DEATH AND RESURRECTION	49
JUDGMENT	65
PURGATORY	81
HEAVEN	97
HELL	113
WHAT DETERMINES DESTINY?	129
OUR RELATIONSHIP WITH THE DEPARTED	145
THE PAROUSIA	161
THE FUTURE OF CHRISTIANITY	177
INDEX TO VOLS. I, II, III, IV	*At end*

I

THE TWO WORLDS

THE whole system of Christian thought and faith rests upon the assumption that there are two worlds or orders of being, one which is visible and one which is invisible. Moreover, the visible world is regarded as temporal, while the invisible world is regarded as eternal. In popular speech these two worlds are often distinguished as " this world " and " the other world," or, sometimes, as " this world " and " the next world." This latter expression is, however, misleading, if it means the next in order of time; it is only that in the sense that it is the next world for us mortals after we leave this. It would not even be correct to use the term " next " spatially, because that other world is not a spatial world at all, though we might say it is really nearest to our own spirits. The relation of this visible to the invisible world is a problem which has vexed the mind of man ever since he realized there were two worlds and began to think about them. For man himself already belongs to both these worlds, and that not merely successively because he at length passes from the one to the other, but because he belongs to them both already, and that intimately, since he is actually compact of them both. For while a part of his nature is visible, namely his body, part of his nature is invisible, namely his spirit, soul or mind, as it may be variously described.

The belief in these two orders of being constitutes

a kind of dualism, and any kind of dualism vexes the human mind, which always craves to reduce things to simplicity and unity; and still more does it present a constant problem to conduct, for the two worlds make competing claims upon man's attention and concern. The world of sense and time is visible, tangible, and presses upon man so immediately that he is sometimes tempted to think that it is the only world that matters or exists. Man may even come to regard belief in another world existing beside or beyond the visible as the product of sheer imagination, probably motived by the desire to escape from the pressure and imperfections of the visible world. Yet to deny the existence of another world beyond that revealed through our senses would involve the rejection of man's most primitive and universal conceptions, as well as of his subtlest self-analysis and most penetrating philosophic thought. Indeed, the dogmatic denial of the existence of the invisible world would deny the reality of all thought, for thought itself belongs to the invisible world. Therefore the common sense of mankind together with philosophic thought hasten to defend the reality of the invisible world, on which the Christian religion builds so much of its faith and hope. But the Christian faith often suffers as much from the defence of the invisible world as from its denial. In our generation, despite the diffusion of education, thought remains somewhat superficial and is rarely sustained, and defence of the invisible world is often made on the claim that a world beyond our sense registration is a matter capable of scientific proof. The very air we breathe is invisible, and yet no one denies its reality and importance. The telescope has revealed to us that there are stars beyond the range of unaided vision, and it is not improbable that there are stars beyond the distance any telescope could reach. We know that there are rays of light at either end of the spectrum which the human eye cannot discern. The existence of an all-pervading ether which neither sense nor instrument reveals has to be assumed by science; and the latest investigations into the constitution of matter would trace even the most solid material to a basis that is itself completely invisible. Therefore it is sometimes claimed that the denial of the invisible world is a piece of dogmatism which science itself has broken down. As a matter of fact, none of these references or discoveries touches the point at issue. These invisibilities are still only matter in a more rarefied and inaccessible form. The point at issue is whether there is a world which is wholly nonmaterial; if so, the existence of such a world is capable neither of sense perception nor of scientific proof. The defence of an invisible world then retreats to what looks like a more intelligent and impregnable position. There is a world which we can all discover for ourselves by reflection and which is non-material: it is the world of thought. Here is a realm immediate to the mind of man, the sphere of so much of his creative activity, and this constitutes a world which is wholly non-material, for thought cannot be seen, weighed or measured. Here surely is sufficient and convincing evidence of an invisible world. If therefore this world of thought and the invisible world which religion proclaims are one and the same, then the existence of such a world very few can doubt, and all thought can be summoned to justify our faith in the unseen. But, in the first place, the non-materiality of the world of thought has been challenged; and, secondly, the complete identification of the world of thought with the invisible spiritual world, with which religion is so concerned, cannot be assumed with safety.

The claim of materialism to reduce the whole of existence to one order, namely, that of the material world, cannot be fully dealt with here; it must suffice to register one or two fatal objections to the materialistic theory of existence. One form of materialism would claim that thought itself is a material thing, because it employs words and images which are ultimately derived from material things. But these are only its instruments; it could be shown that while an image is derived from matter, and the word as uttered employs a material medium, as received by the mind they are not in a material form, neither image nor word is material, and still less is the idea or meaning they convey. Another form of materialism seizes upon the fact that images within the mind are derived from sense perception, while human thought is dependent upon the brain, a physical organ, and its healthy functioning. Christian theology is not concerned to deny our dependence upon sense perceptions and bodily organs; what it does deny is that this dependence makes thought itself material. Even the simplest fact of sense perception, that of vision, is not really reducible to a material process. We know how things outside us excite and stimulate the physical senses and produce the vision of what is without; but although we cannot see without a physical process, and a mechanical reproduction may describe how we see, no merely physical process can explain what it is that sees, and nothing mechanical can ever " see." Still less can it be explained how we call up by memory distant scenes; no examination of a brain, living or dead, can discern its memory; and while we depend upon a healthy brain to think properly, no brain process can actually be conceived as producing ideas within the mind. These two realms of the visible and the invisible are evidently brought into contact through the brain, but how the one is transformed into the other we simply do not know, and cannot indeed conceive how it is possible. Despite the advance of physical science, the subtleties of philosophic thought and the latest psychological researches, we know no more about the mysteries of vision or thought than when man first began to think or inquire. All that we know is that a materialistic explanation is sufficiently ruled out by the fact that materialism is a theory which depends upon non-material thought, and is therefore disproved by the very fact that it is a theory, for a theory is not a material thing.

The existence of these two worlds, and their contact in the mind of man, is so astounding and inexplicable that when he first begins to think man is always inclined to deny the reality of the one side or the other in order to find a solution. And since materialism is invalidated in the very formulation of a system of thought, because it actually denies the reality and validity of thought, many thinkers and some distinguished philosophers take what seems the only alternative, and in the attempt to get rid of this perplexing dualism they deny the reality of the material world. Since, if we are going to think about the world at all, not only the reality but the priority of thought has to be assumed, the theory called idealism is constructed, which holds either that thought is the only reality, or that it is thought that creates the world outside. But on the first supposition the existence of the material world is reduced to a sheer delusion of the human mind, and this condemns human thought as so fundamentally erroneous that it undermines the trustworthiness and therefore the validity of that very world of thought which is claimed to be the only real world. That man creates a whole world of thought, of which the works of art and literature are an expression, need not be denied, but despite the efforts of some to regard this as the only world that matters, few would regard this as the only world that exists, however highly they may appraise its value when compared with the material world. Although man's senses, and still more his ideas, may modify the impact of the external world upon him, and his reaction to it is determined finally by the mental attitude he adopts, hardly anyone would claim that our thought actually creates the world outside us, or if he did could expect to be taken seriously, still less could he order his own life on that assumption. For while it is true that it cannot actually be demonstrated that there exists anything whatsoever outside our own mind, and idealism can challenge materialism to prove that the mind is ever in contact with anything but its own feelings, images and thoughts, no one ever really wants the existence of the outside world to be demonstrated; for it is an immediate intuition of the mind, and while some idealist philosophers seem to have challenged the validity of this intuition, in practice they are forced to act on this assumption; indeed it is largely because certain modern movements have taken idealism seriously and denied the existence of the material world altogether, or some doubtfully sane persons have endeavoured to frame a philosophy of life on the sole reality of their own ego, that many have now wakened up to the pretence and danger of idealism.

These theories, which group themselves under the name of idealism, together with the materialism which they confront, are equally opposed to common sense, and both deny the validity of the very processes of thought by which they come to their conclusions. It may seem ungenerous for Catholic theology to quarrel as much with idealism as it does with materialism, but in doing so it not only takes its stand with man's common sense, but it also refuses to countenance the irrationalism which only proposes theories that ultimately deny the very basis on which they claim to rest. It is necessary, however, to distinguish between strictly philosophical idealism and what is meant by the term in popular speech, where idealism indicates that moral attitude in which ideals are believed to be worthy of trust and pursuit, and capable of realization. It is a minor misfortune, and only adds to our confusion, that the same word should indicate such different things. The extreme error into which idealism has fallen is not only due to the fact that it has denied the reality of the material world, but also that it has made thought a fundamental reality, whereas thought can only be a function of some non-material entity, that non-material entity we call soul or spirit. The existence of the soul within man can no more be proved than can the existence of the outside world. But while the world outside is immediately perceived, the soul has to be inferred by reflection, which is compelled to trace thought to an agent as non-material as its acts : the existence and non-material existence of the soul is therefore inferred from the nature of thought. The unseen world with which Christian theology is concerned is therefore neither the merely invisible, which might be a form of matter invisible only to us, nor is it to be identified merely with the realm of thought. The ultimate reality of the invisible world is spirit, and it consists of personal spiritual beings and their activities, both non-material. Why, then, not employ a positive name, and call it the spiritual world?

But here another confusion emerges which must be cleared up. We use the word spiritual to denote a person whose life is governed by spiritual considerations; "spiritualism" therefore ought to be the name for a theory that the only real world is not so much the realm of thought as activity of a moral order. Such a theory is really involved in the system known as Christian Science, which holds that not only matter but evil does not exist, but that all is mind and good is all. But if we have seen reason to refuse to consider thought to be the sole reality, we need not concern ourselves with the further refinement that good thought is the only reality. No doubt people who accept such ideas generally only mean that mind and goodness are the supreme or ultimate realities; though it should be noted that they often seem content to regard them as abstract and deny their inherence in Personal Spirit, though probably only because they have crude notions of what is meant by personality. But unfortunately for our confusions the word spiritualism has been appropriated not only to the theory that there is a realm of spirits, but to the practice of certain methods through which it is believed they can communicate with us. The attempt has been made to distinguish between moral spirituality and spiritualistic beliefs and researches by the appropriation to the latter of the word "psychic." But even were this distinction observed, Christian theology could not consent to the idea that the morally spiritual is the only reality, for it believes that there are both good and bad spirits, and although man has a spiritual nature which is both invisible and eternal, that it is a nature which may become morally perverted, and that for ever.

Christian theology is therefore committed to a double dualism: it believes in the reality of the spiritual world and it believes equally in the reality of the material world; but it also believes that the spiritual world embraces the moral dualism of good and evil. And this dualism it will not have resolved by mere derivation of one world from another. It does not believe that the material world derives from the spiritual world by a natural process, or came into existence by a moral fall. It believes that the material world was created by God, who is Pure Spirit. Moreover, it believes neither that the material world is evil in itself, nor that evil is eternal or created. Evil is a perversion by the free will of men of that which is in itself good. The problems of creation and of evil have been previously considered from the theoretical point of view, and their discussion must be borne in mind, and cannot here be resumed: what we are now to concern ourselves with in this and the following chapters is the moral purpose of creation and the ultimate destiny of evil. And at this point we are stressing the dualism involved and the difficulties it raises both for thought and practice. Now it must be admitted that the human mind is restive under any form of dualism, and hence the constant effort, even at the sacrifice of all common sense, to relieve the conflict by eliminating one side or the other: denying the reality either of the material or of the spiritual, reducing one to a delusive form of the other, or deriving the one from the other. For if these two worlds are allowed to co-exist and in such difference, then their contact seems to be rendered inconceivable and any transference from one to the other untrustworthy.

Christian theology is, however, by no means content with an absolute dualism; but instead of denying the reality of either side, or simply reconciling them by the device of derivation or by some mere synthesis of thought, it traces both worlds to a Creator and regards the material world as the absolute creation of the Absolute Spirit. But since it believes also that this Absolute Spirit has created dependent creatures like men, who are both material and spiritual, and pure spirits such as the angels, some of whom have fallen, while others remain beyond the possibility of a fall, this not only presents us with a more complicated system than it seems possible to expect that philosophy, with its leanings towards a monistic system, can ever accept, but it raises the question whether such a system as Catholic theology presupposes is anything more than a piece of crude mythology, or if it is more, what proof there is that the system on which theology builds is true. Even if it be sufficiently shown that materialism, on the one hand, and idealism, on the other, are untrue, and if at present there is a movement towards a realism which accepts the reality of both spirit and matter, is the creationist philosophy which Christian theology proposes the only way of escape from an absolute dualism, if that too must be rejected as unintelligible? Now it is admitted by Catholic theology that the doctrine of the creation of the material and spiritual worlds by an Absolute Spirit cannot be proved by reason or science; all that is claimed is that every other explanation can be disproved; further, it is claimed that this explanation of existence has either been revealed through a series of minds whose appeal to divine inspiration, supported as it is by elevated character and extraordinary power, demands consideration; or is deduced from such revelations by the Catholic Church, which claims to inherit a similar inspiration. If this revelation is not accepted, it is held that mankind is left without light on the purpose of life, and is doomed to a series of speculations which only reproduce in other forms theories already disproved. If this revelation is accepted it can then be seen to be actually implied in the basis of both reason and conscience; and in being put to the test by the cultivation of an interior life directed to the invisible and eternal world, it sufficiently validates itself in the experience of its peace and power to enable us to rest upon its promises of a fuller confirmation in the life to come; moreover, nothing but the blissful destiny of the soul, as revealed by Christianity, makes the discipline and suffering of this life tolerable or worth while.

The theoretical difficulty which Christian theology has to face and explain is why it was necessary for there to be two worlds: why, in short, the material world and mankind were ever created. The only answer that can be given is that the material world was created in order to develop and discipline created finite souls so that they might be brought into union with the Infinite Creator Spirit. The existence of the material world and the temporal life of human beings were designed solely for the invisible world and eternal life. What confirmation is there of such a meaning and purpose in this material and temporal life? First it may be noted that there is a certain analogy between the conception of the material world as created for the development of souls and the doctrine of evolution. At first sight it looks an astounding claim that the material world, with its vast measures of space and time, should exist solely for some purpose connected with the human soul. But even the most naturalistic interpretation of evolution has to assume something very like it; for even if that interpretation regards the material world as actually producing human souls, that must be assumed to be its ultimate purpose, so far as a material world can be regarded as capable of having a purpose; anyhow, without the emergence of the human soul the material world would be left unexplained, because there would be no one to explain it. This same naturalistic doctrine of evolution must regard the immense spatial and temporal existence of the universe as absolutely necessary to the production of the human soul; and the only difference that theology would demand at this point is not the denial of evolution altogether, but that the material world was the instrument that the Creator used for the shaping of the soul of man. This immense measurement and these enormous time conditions indicate not so much the difficulty of the task the Creator has undertaken as the immensity of the value of the soul and of the glory for which it is being prepared. Yet if, as it is held, angels could be created in a moment perfect beings, it might well be wondered why the creation of man has taken all this preparation and man should be created with capabilities yet to be perfected. The explanation must be that man's destiny is so much higher than that of the angels, which indeed Catholic theology teaches; for while angels have the vision of God, man is made for union with God, which moreover cannot be effected without man's own choice and co-operation. The acceptance of such a revelation certainly demands faith, but

THE TWO WORLDS

if it is not accepted, then we are left with a problem that is gigantic, insoluble, and tragic, namely, that the material world has produced something non-material, in itself a totally unscientific notion, for how the one can produce the other is simply inconceivable. Further, it has produced conscious personalities, whose purpose is hidden and whose destiny is dark, and who are faced with the contemplation of that fact on the one side, and on the other with the reflection that they have emerged as minds from the mindless, as conscious beings from the unconscious, whose life is left without any other meaning than to realize the meaninglessness of existence. This explanation is not only tragic, it is idiotic; and it is as irrational as it is hopeless. Thus we are shut up to the faith which alone gives us light, and if we will accept this faith enough is made clear to enable us to go on to discover how temporal life is meant to train us for immortal life, our physical bodies are meant to waken our souls into consciousness, the invisible world is meant to reveal the invisible world, and our earthly experience is meant to create the desire for God and prepare us for its realization.

The difficulties in this scheme are its absence of scientific demonstration, the pressure and immediacy of the present world of sense and time, and the failure of imagination to anticipate in sufficient degree that spiritual existence which would make this present existence worth while. Concerning the question of scientific proof, in addition to what has been said, it need only be pointed out that it is to demand the impossible; science cannot demonstrate anything beyond the material, for that is its only concern. But philosophy can then be brought in to show that science itself can give no explanation of the existence of the material world, while, even for its purpose, it cannot ignore the existence of the invisible world of thought. Then religion comes in to show that by thought alone philosophy cannot attain to a comprehensive theory or to a fundamental explanation; its theories run out into antinomies, each one of them in the end contradicting the very basis on which it builds, and invalidating the position from which it starts. It therefore has to wait for further light to come to the mind of man from without. This light is, however, not wholly external, for it confirms and supplements the natural light of reason and answers the need of man for just such a revelation. Revelation, therefore, does not contradict science or philosophy, it rather completes them both; and if either science or philosophy rejects that completion, then they fall inevitably into scepticism and pessimism, and eventually contradict their own premises. It is therefore by the light of revelation that we must live, if we are going to live at all. But the light of revelation is only an intensification of the light of reason already given us, while the light of experience confirms the light of faith. To turn from the light of revelation means in the end putting out all light whatsoever.

The predominance and pressure of the invisible world is very largely a moral decision. This world may seem to us immediate and all-engaging, and consequently we may choose to live for the things of sense alone and as if this present world were all. But this conclusion is a perversion of the pressure of the material world and the lessons to be learned from it. The most immediate reality is our own souls, for only by the soul can the material world be discerned. And if we stop for a moment to think we can soon discern that the pressure of this world is intended to waken our souls within, since even the material world means nothing until the soul wakens; and then, when the soul, conscious of itself, looks back upon the material world, it sees that it is not self-explained: it could not create the soul and cannot satisfy it. So, by yielding to the thought and desire thus awakened, the soul rises to the idea of a Spirit, greater than the world, like to but greater than the soul, who must have created the world and must have created it for the purpose of arousing the soul. The very pressure of the material world therefore awakens us to the existence of another order of reality within, and to seek its cause in the only reality sufficient to explain both, namely God. If we choose to ignore the voice of our own souls, try to satisfy ourselves with the material world and live for temporal life alone, we shall bring down upon ourselves darkness, depression and defeated desire. If, however, we rise to the thought of God, and if we use this world to extract from it eternal treasure, living for eternity in time, then we shall find that the material world is a help to us, that all things can be turned to the perfecting of the soul, and that temporal life becomes so full of significance that it can be endured, and even welcomed, as the necessary way to the invisible and the eternal.

The discovery of the vastness of the universe, the immense extension of time, and the multitudes of souls that have sojourned in this world, may at first seem confusing and cause perplexity; but further thought will see in these things only indications of the glory of God, the splendour of our own destiny, and the necessity of human fellowship. The majesty of the material universe is meant to assure us of the far greater majesty of Him who made it; the immense stretches of time are meant to assure us of the value of eternity; and not only our fellowship with souls now existing, but our inheritance from the thoughts, the achievements and victories of the past illuminate the treasures of wisdom and knowledge that are hidden in God, and prepare us for the communion of saints through which our inheritance in Him will be increased for us. We need these vast stretches of time to prepare us for eternity; we need contact with our fellows to deepen our personalities, and we need close communion with the whole redeemed community in heaven and on earth to make our union with God wide and rich.

A further difficulty may, however, be felt to remain when, in the light of these immensities, we consider the brevity of our personal lives here on earth, which seems to provide insufficient preparation for eternity. But it needs to be remembered that our temporal life comes to us already enriched from the past; it is further enriched by our contact with others living around us. None of us really wants life to last much longer than its allotted span; as life becomes more complex and personality more conscious, it often becomes just as much as we can endure, and indeed we can only endure it, sometimes for a day, because of the hope of eternity beyond. Moreover, the eternity with which this temporal life is associated is not simply time extended to infinity, it is rather experience intensified to the infinite; and not only can this life be lived in the light of eternity, but eternity can itself be experienced by the way in which this life is lived. The world, then, within which we are now living is in closest contact with the other world; it awakens us to the existence of that other world; it is meant to train us for that other world. The dualism of the two worlds is therefore resolved by their creation by the same Creator, the moral subjection of the material to the spiritual, the preparation of the temporal for the eternal.

II

BODY, SOUL AND SPIRIT

IT is in man that the two worlds of matter and spirit, so utterly different in their nature and mode, not only come into contact, but enter into the closest possible union, a union which is necessary to the very existence of man. Because of this contact, there takes place within man that astonishing process by which material things are made the basis of abstract thought. The process involves both their dependence and their difference; for, on the one hand, the most abstract thought reveals to analysis its perpetual dependence upon material images and physical sensations, and yet, on the other hand, not only does the abstract nature of thought reveal a complete difference from anything material, but the simplest act of perception involves a process which cannot be physically explained. It is because of the abstract nature of human thought and the psychical element in perception that we infer the existence of that purely non-material entity in man which is called the soul. It may seem disappointing to fervent believers in spiritual realities thus to define the soul in a merely negative way and to be content with saying that it is non-material; and it may seem precarious to make the soul's existence a mere inference from argument; they would think it better to take the far more challenging and confident position and claim outright that the soul is a spiritual substance, of whose existence we are directly conscious by introspection. But while the scholastic theology does define the soul as a spiritual substance, the word substance, unfortunately, has in popular use mostly a material connotation; and that we have no positive conception of what a purely spiritual entity may be can be seen from the fact that the very word spirit has material associations, however refined, for, of course, it originally meant breath or wind. But one of the advantages of the scholastic attitude is to be found in its fundamental modesty and its willingness frankly to face all the facts which its opponents bring forward; for while it admits that material things are immediately perceived, and no person in his right mind feels called upon to prove their existence, it denies that the existence of the soul can be immediately perceived by itself; and although there must be a soul to think, and even to perceive, it needs the process of thought to establish the existence of the soul; in short, it is an intellectual inference. On the other hand, from the nature of that intellectual process, the nature of the soul can be inferred with entire certainty; for although perception is the perception of material things, perception itself is not material, and although the most abstract reasoning still depends upon material images, reasoning is an entirely non-material process. Therefore, from the nature of its own highest activities the soul is able to infer its own existence and that its nature is non-material. This inference will only seem precarious to those who do not recognize the nature of thought and the certainty with which the inference can be made; and although doubtless primitive man, and most modern men, employ this process of inference in an unreflective way and do not stay to analyse it, nothing is gained by claiming that man has an immediate intuition of the soul, when it can be objected that from the very names given to the soul primitive man inferred its existence only by analogy, and when modern analytical thinkers deny that they have any immediate perception of their own souls. But to thought, able to analyse its own process and to recognize its own nature, it is obvious that, however much thought may depend upon material objects, it must have a subject; there cannot be thoughts without a thinker, and the nature of thought shows the nature of the thinker.

But while the scholastic theology admits that the soul of man depends upon the senses of the body, and their contact with the external material world for its being aroused into activity, and for the knowledge it comes to possess, it maintains that the soul is not only utterly different from the body, but is essentially independent of it; so that the soul is in its nature like God, who is pure spirit. And it is on these dual facts that there is explained the necessity for the soul having an earthly life and a bodily experience, and there can be inferred the spiritual destiny for which this experience was designed to train the soul. For not only can the soul be discerned to be non-material, because of its higher powers of abstraction and reasoning, but it can be discerned to be spiritual, because it reasons to the existence of God, and craves communion with Him as its own natural completion. In the highest of its activities it must therefore be like God, for without likeness to God it cannot have communion with Him. The human soul is therefore a spirit, and because it is a spirit it is like to God, partaking of the same nature, only in a finite instead of in an infinite degree.

It is not surprising that in the Scriptures man's soul is also called a spirit, which is declared to be the very nature of God, for " God is Spirit." But it is somewhat confusing that while the terms soul

BODY, SOUL AND SPIRIT

and spirit are sometimes used as if they were interchangeable, they are sometimes used as if they referred to distinct entities. St. Paul's enumeration of our "whole spirit, soul and body," seems to imply that the spirit is as distinct from the soul as the soul is from the body, and his enumeration has more than once been thought to sanction a tripartite psychology. In the early centuries of the Church a whole religious system was founded on their distinction, for a type of Gnosticism arose which distinguished two types of men, the psychical and the spiritual; and, indeed, this distinction is made by the apostle himself, who compares the spiritual man to the disparagement of the merely psychical man, or the "natural" man, as our English versions somewhat unfortunately render the term. But the Gnostic system went farther than making this distinction: it believed that the distinction was due to the fact that most men possessed only souls, while a few possessed also spirits. The Church theologians rejected this conclusion, which they regarded as a mistaken deduction from the apostle's language. It is not as easy to show that the apostle's language does not sanction the Gnostic interpretation as it is to see why the Church took up this position and what a defence on behalf of our common humanity it has thus made; for the Gnostic psychology would compel us to admit that there are human beings who are incapable of spirituality, because they are not spirits, and that to be made capable of spirituality they must have added to them a third entity, a spiritual substance that is not theirs by creation or right. It would, therefore, have to be inferred of a great number, and perhaps of the majority of mankind, that they were not naturally immortal, and that, for all their mental capacities, some men were incapable of spirituality; in short, that the regenerate belonged to a higher race and constituted a distinct species. It must be admitted that the language of the apostle Paul often seems to provide a basis for such ideas, and even to demand this interpretation; but a closer examination of his writings shows that this is not so. The "natural," or, as the word can be transliterated, the "psychic" man is the man who has chosen to concern himself with the higher activities of his soul, but only in so far as they concern himself, and without any reference to the end of his being, which was designed for spiritual communion with God. St. Paul certainly teaches that without being touched by the Spirit of God this natural or psychic man cannot discern spiritual realities. But this is not because he does not possess the faculty, but because he has deliberately chosen not to use it until it has become atrophied; he has turned away from the things of God until this has become the habit of his soul. The touch of the Spirit of God upon man's soul does not generate a spirit within him; it re-generates his soul and restores its spiritual function. It will therefore be seen that a tripartite psychology, or the theory that man consists of three separate substances, body, soul and spirit, is a false deduction from a distinction which was not meant to be substantial; and, therefore, that St. Paul agrees with the rest of the Scriptures, which refer at one time to man's soul and at another time to his spirit in such a way that we must assume that it is the same substance which is being referred to, but perhaps now this and now the other aspect of it is being emphasized. We have therefore to conclude that man is body and soul, but that his soul is also spirit, and therefore immortal and capable of, nay, demanding, communion with God for its true functioning. The soul of man, therefore, needs regeneration in order to be spiritual, but not in order to be a spirit; it is that by its natural creation.

The question arises, however, whether modern theology would not free itself from the constant confusion which occurs from the popular use of these scriptural terms if it adopted the nomenclature body, mind and spirit, letting mind take the place of the soul in St. Paul's three-fold analysis. But before we can do this with any confidence, we must be certain that what is meant by the modern terminology of the word mind can be identified with St. Paul's use of the word soul. Now it is from the higher activities of the mind, namely, by intellectual reasoning, that the existence of the soul is demonstrated; it is from its highest activities that the nature of the soul is inferred; and yet constantly in Scripture the soul is used with the obvious connotation, not of man's mental powers so much as of his moral character. Hence the soul is spoken of as being lost, and even destroyed, which certainly does not mean that man retains no mental powers, or that he goes out of existence; it means he has lost his moral powers, his freedom, and, in the case of final perdition, the possibility of coming into communion with God. Therefore it seems unwise to equate mind and soul; indeed, it would be more in accordance with modern usage to make the triple division body, mind and soul, understanding, as modern terminology generally does, that the soul is the spiritual substance of man, and mind merely one of its functions. It must be remembered, however, that while man has a spirit, this does not itself guarantee that he will be spiritual in the moral sense of that word; that he will recognize his natural likeness to God and attempt to become morally like God through communion with Him. Therefore it seems best to employ the Scriptural terms body, soul and spirit alongside such modern terms as mind, reason and conscience, leaving their connotation and reference to be defined as the occasion demands; it is often a source of confusion, but it would make confusion worse confounded to attempt at present a greater simplicity, or to identify the modern term mind with the Scriptural term soul. That was possible when scholastic terminology was dominant, for under that usage soul was more equivalent to the modern term mind, especially as that now includes the unconscious mind. And in one classic phrase this usage is retained where it is important to recognize its approximation to the modern connotation of the term mind, namely, in the Athanasian Creed, where to Christ there is ascribed a "rational soul;" the adjective "rational" emphasizing the identification with mind, and the word soul certainly not to be regarded as the personal self, which in Christ is to be identified with the pre-existing Person of the Eternal Word, the Second Person in the Blessed Trinity.

We are to conclude therefore that man has not both a soul *and* a spirit. He has a soul which is *also* a spirit, one non-material substance, its soul functions looking downward towards the body, its spirit functions looking upward to God; soul not being quite identifiable with mind, not even when mind includes not only the intellect, but the affections and the will, as well as the unconscious processes by which it comes into closest contact with the body; for in modern terminology soul is sometimes used to denote the very self or ego, the subject of the whole personality; while in Scriptural terminology the soul is often used to denote the moral character. There is no doubt, however, that the mind is a most important function of the soul, and that through its mental processes the soul exercises its supreme spiritual activities; nevertheless mental processes of the most abstract kind can be exercised without spiritual aim, and indeed not only to the neglect of its spiritual functions and the destruction of its moral harmony, but in order to deny the very existence of the soul.

In the Pauline enumeration of body, soul and spirit, soul may here approximate to our modern term mind; but his adjective " soulish " or psychical hardly means the same as our adjective intellectual; save in so far as intellectuality may be puffed up with pride, maintain its independence of God, and itself be used to shut out all spiritual appeal by sophistry, as unfortunately it so often is in brilliant and irreligious minds. The Pauline enumeration was, however, intended, as the context shows, not to sanction a psychological trichotomy, but to indicate that all these departments of our personality were capable of complete sanctification, thus providing a necessary correction of any idea that the body or the mind of man are in any sense essentially evil. Indeed, the Pauline enumeration of body, soul and spirit seems to indicate their combination rather than their difference; and not only to allow that soul and spirit are one substance, but that this substance is also in the closest union with the body. Man is not a soul with a body; man is soul and body in substantial union.

Here a much more important consideration than that of definition now awaits us; for the question is now raised why the spiritual substance of man's soul was ever united with that material substance we call the human body. Now here, as we have already seen, Catholic theology comes closer to the

BODY, SOUL AND SPIRIT

demands of modern thought than many other types of philosophy, in conceding that the soul is in close dependence upon the body. It recognizes that the soul depends entirely for its conscious and intellectual life upon its union with the body. It is through the senses that it is made aware of the existence of the material world, but it is also from the material provided by the senses that it becomes conscious of itself as a soul, and rises to the thought of God. Catholic theology, therefore, in distinction from idealistic philosophy, does not believe that the soul starts with innate ideas, or that thought is the only reality, but believes that the soul is dependent for all its ideas upon the contribution of the senses, and that there is nothing in the intellect which was not first given by the senses. It is therefore not perplexed by the fact that the moment the senses cease to act, as they do in sleep or under the action of some drug, consciousness ceases and the intellect remains a blank. Catholic theology, unlike idealistic philosophy, can therefore accept the common facts of our mental life and the researches of modern psychological science without alarm. Nevertheless it does not admit the conclusions of materialistic philosophy, which would infer from these facts that, because the soul depends for its knowledge upon the senses, the soul is to be identified with consciousness, and therefore ceases to exist when it is unconscious, and apart from its knowledge possesses no power. These facts constitute no difficulty for Catholic theology, for it is by reflecting upon them that it arrives at the conclusion that the chief concern of the soul is moral character, and that its union with the body is given to it not merely for the accumulation of knowledge, nor simply in order to make it an instrument for perfect reasoning, valuable as these may be, but in order to gain for the soul a moral quality which can be eternally fixed. If the union of the soul with the body were simply for the purpose of gaining knowledge and intellectual power, then the inequalities of life, especially as they are dependent upon bodily conditions, such as the right functioning of the brain, would affect not only this life, but determine our eternal destiny. But it can be readily discerned that intellectual capacity does not determine moral quality, and that many who are deficient in the power of abstract reasoning nevertheless can attain characters of moral beauty and strength. This attainment is therefore open to souls where sense perception has been dull and intellect even deficient; indeed, the very difficulties caused by sense disorganization through sickness or infirmity, the recognized limitations of intellectual life, have, in many cases, obviously been the means of calling out greater moral effort in order to rise superior to limitations and defects. This recognition, however, only brings us in sight of another difficulty: that there are forms of sense imperfection and types of mental deficiency which certainly seem to produce immoral behaviour. There are criminal types which we have every reason to suspect are due to physical and mental deficiency, certain forms of insanity manifest themselves in immoral behaviour, and certain forms of imbecility in immoral propensity. But here we have to distinguish carefully between immoral behaviour and moral responsibility, for which we must not only leave it to the Judge of all the earth, Who sees all things, to reward all men justly, but we can ourselves easily recognize that the actual moral quality of the soul is not to be equated with moral behaviour. Moral character, namely that which has a fixed and eternal moral value, depends upon the proportion between a man's moral illumination and his obedience to it. A man who has had little moral instruction, whose environment has been deleterious, and whose temptations have been strong, may actually have exerted greater moral power and, therefore, gained greater merit than many a person who has lived a morally much superior life, but who has had far better conditions. This is why the Christian religion has never been content to identify spiritual capacity with moral attainment. Not only does much depend, in that proportion to which we have referred, upon the effort which had actually to be made, but also on the motive by which it was made. Therefore the soul with a very inferior moral code, or the soul actually in bondage to sin from which it has never been wholly able to break away, nevertheless, because of its recognition of its dependence upon God and its desire for Him, may carry out of this world a much greater moral potentiality than a soul much more upright and successful; and it may find that its efforts, which in this world seemed to have ended only in failure, have, nevertheless, laid up for it a treasure in heaven much greater than that awaiting the soul whose moral attainments have been easier. These considerations partly explain the emphasis laid, neither upon understanding nor upon behaviour, as decisive for the final destiny of the soul, but upon faith; though, as these same considerations demand, neither upon faith as a mere trust in God's mercy to make up for our deficiencies, nor upon faith as a kind of superior theological understanding or superior spiritual vision, but upon "faith working by love"; that is, upon faith as intense moral desire. Therefore it needs to be borne in mind that the real and eternal gain that the soul makes by its union with the body is not to be identified either with intellectual brilliance or moral attainment, but with moral effort, and still more with moral desire, for it is this latter which determines a man's potential capacity for God, and this is the treasure man is here on earth to gain.

Man's chief business in life, therefore, is to preserve the hierarchy of body, soul and spirit. If he lives for carnal pleasures only, and disregards the claims of mental life, he sins against his own soul, he goes against the light of reason, frustrates the purpose of earthly experience, and denies the aim of his existence. If, however, he lives purely for æsthetic satisfaction and mental exercise he sins against his spirit and denies the appeal of his conscience; and his sin is worse than that of the merely carnal, because his æsthetic senses and his intellectual reasonings ought to have wakened a clearer conviction of the nature of God and a craving for His holiness. This is why the purely æsthetic and merely intellectual types more often fall far lower than the merely careless and purely carnal: the artist who is nothing more can fall into the most degraded perversions, and the intellectual who is nothing more may turn into a cynical mocker at faith. Even the desire for a moral life, in so far as that is motived merely to stand well with one's fellows or even merely to be at peace with oneself, would be a still greater sin against the end of life; because the dependence of our ideals upon divine inspiration, and the gratitude for grace received, should make us only the more conscious of how much we depend upon God for that communion with Infinite Holiness which alone satisfies moral aspiration. It is spiritual and philosophical considerations like these which enable us to understand our Lord's declaration in the Gospels that the harlot and publican go into the kingdom of heaven before the scribe and the Pharisee, and why He thanked His Father that the greatest things had been revealed not to the "wise and prudent," but to those who are babes, and who know it and admit it; for the scribe and Pharisee, although they were undoubtedly more moral than the harlot and the publican, ought only to have been the more grateful and humble, instead of proud and unforgiving; and an intellect that was not blinded by pride would itself recognize its dependence upon God, and know itself to be but a babe in the matter of true knowledge.

It can be equally seen that not only does the soul depend upon the body, and the spirit upon the mind, but that this dependence is in no sense an evil, but always provides man with an impulse towards good. The incompatibility between spirit and matter is psychological and not moral; indeed, the pressure of the body upon the soul is never the cause of carnality: the moment the soul surrenders to the body, the body rebels. The surrender to passion creates in it appetites which immediately disorganize and eventually destroy the body. Therefore the body cannot be blamed for dragging the soul down; it clearly warns the soul against any such abdication of its position. Neither, again, do mental occupations constitute an inevitable temptation against spirituality, for the moment æsthetic appreciation throws off moral purpose it begins to deteriorate, denies its own standards, and ends in a perverse love of ugliness; while intellectual brilliance, if it denies the Godward reference of all true thought, has to deny its own basis, finds itself with declining belief in the possibility of attaining truth, and the mind is at last plunged into pessimistic conclusions involving the most dreadful darkness and misery.

Therefore we can say that the soul is united to a

body, in the first place, in order to increase its moral potentiality ; the spirit is to gain its own soul, that is, a moral character. In the second place, the body is there to make it more difficult for the soul to sink, and the operations of mind are to prevent the spirit centring upon itself. It has been a tempting speculation to regard the bodily experience of the soul as necessary to give it personality, to mark off, as it were, from the general soul substance a portion in which individuality can be developed ; but, attractive as such speculations are to modern pantheistic notions, they are forbidden to Catholic theology, which holds the spirit of man to be, not an emanation from the Spirit of God, but a creation, a spirit distinct from, though like to, His own, and regards every individual soul as separately created by God. This is certainly more in accordance with the conceptions of the nature of spirit, gives greater dignity to man, and a higher purpose to earthly life. For Catholic theology holds that angels, who are pure spirits, and have mighty intellects, were created perfect by God without any dependence upon a bodily organism or need of an earthly experience ; so that the body cannot be necessary to individuality, or a life upon earth to the attainment of knowledge. Therefore the union of man's soul with a body, and his probation of earthly life, must be to gain for him something superior to the angelic nature ; and such we are allowed to believe is the purpose of man's creation : he was made a little lower than the angels only in order that through the attainment of a moral capacity, which should be due not only to divine endowment but to his own choice, he might be prepared for what no angel can ever attain, namely, union with God.

With our investigations in mind, we can therefore regard the human spirit as sent into this world to acquire capacity and character, which is precisely what the Scriptures mean when they talk about gaining the soul. It is not to be thought, however, that the eternal gain we gather from our earthly experience is something, as it were, simply squeezed out of material things, æsthetic perception and intellectual life, and that these things are therefore in themselves valueless and temporary. The doctrine of the resurrection of the body assumes that the body is not a mere instrument to be thrown aside when the work by which it is accomplished is completed; still less does it mean that æsthetic perception and intellectual creation have no contribution to make to the eternal gain of the soul. Just as the intellect does not merely add something to material things so much as discerns the nonmaterial element in them, and thus rises through creation to the thought of the Creator, so æsthetic perception gathers from material things, as it were sacramentally, the vision of that beauty of God which is holiness; and so also does true intellectuality abstract from the greatest achievements of thought the intellectual vision of God; so that the true theologian is always bound to be also a mystic. Mere materialism, mere æstheticism, mere intellectualism are only possible if the mind deliberately blinds itself to the spirituality really immanent in the particular objects of perception, appreciation, and conception. Indeed, it may be said that it is the senses and the intellect which make an abstraction from total reality, and the soul which embraces the heart of reality; so that to remain content with the lower levels of mere material objects, or even with abstract thought, is the false abstraction, which that true abstraction which is the supreme function of the soul, should reveal. The soul, by rising above these things, does not, however, throw them aside in gaining from them vision, capacity and desire: it elevates them to their true significance. Not only the material world of nature, but the finest productions of human art and the greatest creations of pure intellect mean something more to the spiritual soul than to merely material or merely intellectual comprehension; so that the spiritual soul will sometimes extract from the works of some great artist or poet more than their creator himself could see.

Thus the union of the soul with the body is neither necessary, for angels could be created without bodies; nor is it a fall on the part of the soul itself from pure spirituality, tempted by material things; nor is it a merely temporary device for securing the awakening of the soul; still less is it a moral drag or hindrance. It is the good purpose of the Creator to bring man to a higher state of existence than is open to any created spirit such as an angel, namely, into such a union with Himself as belongs only eternally, naturally, and properly to His only begotten Son; for man was created in Christ Jesus for the purpose of being perfectly conformed to His image, that he might become a partaker in the Divine nature. That is the meaning of our earthly career, planned by the Divine grace, motived by the Eternal Love, not for His need, but for our sake; for His glory, indeed, but only for His glory in so far as that means that we shall give glory to Him when we ourselves share His glory.

III

IMMORTALITY

NEXT to the existence of God, the immortality of the soul is the most fundamental of all human beliefs; for without the assumption of its truth it is difficult to find any rational meaning or ethical worth in human existence. And although the existence of God and the immortality of the soul are, apart from revelation, only an inference of human thought, yet with varying conceptions of their nature, until the rise of modern scepticism, they have been deep-seated and almost universal convictions of the human mind. Both beliefs are due to mental argument, whether of a simple or abstruse character, but it is an argument which, once man begins to think, is almost inevitably followed. In both cases, although the argument is only an inference, it is strengthened by the consideration that the denial of either belief is not only impossible to prove, but immediately involves us in absurdities. The existence of God is an inference from our observation of the world; the existence of the soul is an inference from the fact that we observe the world, and so recognize our distinction from it; in short, the existence of the soul is inferred from its activities. Although it might be imagined that the very contiguity of ourselves and the fact that our souls are involved in our own activities would make the existence of the soul our first conviction, and therefore one held with the greater certainty, it would appear that the existence of God comes to be believed in

IMMORTALITY

first; and this is because we become engaged with the problem of the external world, and come to believe that it must have been made by someone, before we turn to reflect upon the nature of thought, which frames such arguments, and so become convinced of the soul, which must be the agent of such thought. For the soul is, as it were, more deeply hidden within its own acts, because they are, like itself, purely spiritual; whereas the Spirit of God is not so involved in the material movement and physical life of the world, which to the slightest thought always demands a cause different in nature from itself. Nevertheless, once reflection is awakened, the existence and nature of the soul are seen to be so implied in the activity and nature of thought, that it becomes more difficult to deny the existence of the soul than the existence of God. When, therefore, reflection is pursued apart from the confirmation of revelation, the soul comes to occupy a more fundamental concern than that of God, as may be seen from the interests of a philosophical race like the Greeks; and even modern philosophy is inclined to make the existence of the soul the starting point of thought, and to rest content with an assurance of immortality, while remaining unconvinced or less concerned about the existence of God; though whether it shows a deeply philosophical mind to be able to rest in such a position, or whether to attempt to do so must not in the end destroy philosophy itself, is at least questionable.

The intensely reflective thought of the Greek mind became absorbed in demonstrating the existence of the soul, and, discerning from the nature of its highest acts that, in contrast to the body, it was a purely spiritual entity, soon arrived at the conviction of its immortality, arguing from its absolute simplicity and spirituality that it was indestructible

IMMORTALITY

and incorruptible. The doctrine of the immortality of the soul therefore owes much to the Greek mind, and its defence still draws upon the arguments it employed; a fact which has led some Christians to underrate their value, and even to question whether the immortality of the soul is a Christian doctrine. At the same time, Greek thought about the soul was inclined to induce belief as much in its pre-existence as in its continuance after death, and thus found itself unable to give a satisfactory explanation of the necessity or meaning of earthly experience. And although the primitive Greek mind had earlier arrived at a belief in the existence of God, it seemed less concerned with God than with the soul, and so arrived very slowly and uncertainly at any idea of His nature or unity.

The religion of the Hebrews was so dominated by its revelation of the majestic and transcendent nature of God, and the record of numerous Divine commands concerning daily life so developed their practical interests, that the Hebrew mind gave little thought to the nature of the soul, and even seemed relatively unconcerned in personal immortality, until a surprisingly late period. An impression has been derived from these facts, which is, however, incorrect, namely, that the Hebrews did not come to believe in the immortality of the soul until they had come into contact with Greek speculation. Rather, they seem to have shared with earlier Greek, and with all primitive thought, the belief that the soul continues to exist after the dissolution of the body, but in a shadowy, depleted, and aimless existence. Concern for a higher kind of immortality arose through the intense experience of personal communion with God which was developed under Hebrew worship and prophecy; and the conviction began to take shape that this communion could not cease

IMMORTALITY

with this life, but indeed must be carried to a higher stage, if the desires of the soul and God's purposes for it were to be realized.

Eastern religious thought never arrived at so clear a conception as the Greeks in regard to the soul, or as the Hebrews in regard to God, the idea of God remaining largely impersonal; the soul, although regarded as an emanation of the divine essence, was believed to pass through many existences, some of them even sub-human, therefore remaining almost without subjective identity, and with no purpose in earthly experience save to discover its delusive separation from the Divine, and then to seek reabsorption, and apparently lose individuality, and so any consciousness of existence.

From the primitive conception of a shadowy life beyond the grave Egyptian thought developed an idea of immortality which is practically a perpetuation of earthly life, though differentiated into one of reward or penalty according to earthly conduct and condition. It is interesting to note the concentration upon the after-life which distinguishes Egyptian religion, its much less concern for clear conceptions of God, or for the religious aspect of life beyond the grave, the gods remaining very little distinguished from the more aristocratic human souls, and even being confused with forms of animal life. Consequently, Egyptian religion contributed practically nothing to the general religious development of mankind, save in so far as it was adopted by the mystery cults which swarmed in the late Hellenic and early Roman Empire, though perhaps some influence may be traceable in some elements of modern Spiritualism; in both cases, however, it is exotic, Egyptian religion remaining on the whole as embalmed and mummified as its method of

IMMORTALITY

burial; a perpetual warning against a merely spiritistic religion.

Christianity assumes the almost universal idea of the continuance of the soul after death, taking over from Greek thought its clear conception of the spiritual nature of the soul, and of the survival of its personal identity and intellectual powers, combining with this a strong conviction that the state of the life thus continued is determined by the character gained on earth, which is fixed by a process of judgment after death; though this apparently owes nothing to Egyptian thought, but is probably to be traced to Zoroastrian conceptions, though in this case, as with any Greek influence, only as it had been already assimilated and shaped by the Hebrew mind, under a dominant religious concern for the continuance and consummation of communion with God. The developed theology of the Church adopted more openly and definitely the Greek conception of the nature of the soul, and the Greek arguments for its continued existence based upon its spirituality and simplicity.

The Church's theology would therefore repudiate the tendency of some small sects and a few theologians to make the immortality of the soul forfeited by the Fall and now dependent upon spiritual regeneration through faith in Christ. Although admitting that immortality is God's gift to man, the Church's theology teaches that this gift will never be withdrawn, and the scriptural texts adduced against a natural immortality it regards as wrongly interpreted, owing to a confusion between their reference to moral destruction and the death of the soul, and the idea of the annihilation of the spirit. These ideas will have to be given a closer examination under another heading, but meanwhile it can be noted how Catholic theology at

IMMORTALITY

this point, as in so many others, defends the dignity and rights of the natural order, and refuses to sanction a division among human beings which would amount to a difference of species, with all the disastrous possibilities that would hold for our estimate of many of our fellow-creatures.

To the surprise of some modern concern Christian theology has been content to rest on an admittedly inferential argument with regard to the immortality of the soul, as it has been satisfied to rest content with admittedly negative proofs for the existence of God; but this is because, on the latter point, the natural basis has been confirmed by the supernatural revelation of God through the Incarnation of the Eternal Word in Christ; and on the matter of immortality, because of the definite teaching and promise of Christ concerning His resumed and consummated personal relationship in the life to come with the souls He has redeemed; but particularly because that teaching has been confirmed by the astounding revelation of His own Resurrection, which is not only a supernatural revelation of continued spirituality, but of transcendent spiritual power, manifested in raising His body from the corruption of the grave and transforming it into a glorious instrument for communication with His disciples; immortality being now for us no longer a mere inference, or an invisible reality belonging to an incommunicable sphere, but an episode inserted into earthly history, a fact upon the plane of physical demonstration.

The philosophical apologetic for the immortality of the soul must therefore seem to the convinced Christian somewhat otiose, and is only employed to remove fundamental objections in the way of an approach of an unbeliever to the consideration of the Christian faith. But, in addition, the Christian

IMMORTALITY

believer remains somewhat cold or suspicious in the face of modern attempts to establish the continued existence of the human soul as a scientific fact by means of communications with the departed. This is for various reasons; as far as his own faith is concerned, he is content with the promises of Christ, confirmed so wonderfully by His glorious Resurrection, and with the higher experiences of prayer in which he believes he already tastes eternal life here in this world. In addition, it is one of the fundamental positions of the scholastic theology that the soul is only able to communicate with other souls through the medium of the body, and therefore that departed souls cannot naturally communicate with us unless by some supernatural means. This allows for the possibility of the communion of saints, but this operates normally through the medium of prayer, although sometimes, but then miraculously, by visions or verbal communications. Therefore it is in accordance with the Christian attitude to commend to a person unable to believe in Christ's Resurrection, or who is without mystical experience, that he should fall back upon the Greek argument of immortality as able to be inferred from the very nature of the soul, strengthened, as this can be, by general moral and theological considerations, rather than embark upon the widely deceptive, highly dubious, and possibly dangerous methods of modern Spiritualism.

The alleged evidence of Spiritualism and the instinctively Christian attitude towards it deserve, however, further consideration. It is immensely difficult to sum up with any claim to scientific impartiality the vast mass of material which has been accumulated in the endeavour to discover actual evidence of the survival of human personality by means of communication with departed souls. A great quantity of the material obtained through mediumistic séances must be dismissed as consciously fraudulent, unconsciously deceptive, or highly doubtful. There remains a residuum which, however wonderful, may be explained as due to subconscious activity; but whatever may be covered by that explanation, it leaves open the possibility that the subconscious may be the medium of communication with departed souls. At this point, therefore, we have to try to separate between the powers of the subconscious mind to communicate with minds living on earth, by means of what is called telepathy, and the communication of knowledge which it is beyond the power of the human mind, as we know it, to obtain. But here we are faced with a double difficulty. On the one hand, telepathy can hardly be claimed as yet to have been established as a scientific fact to the conviction of all those who have experimented with it and can be counted as trained observers and impartial witnesses. And, on the other hand, we do not know whether the unconscious mind of living persons may not have more powers than have actually been classed under the category of telepathy. If we knew that telepathy was a fact, and if we knew the limits of its range, then we should know that everything beyond it must be referred to the activity of discarnate spirits. Now everything belonging to this extra-telepathic region sorts itself into two categories: statements we can check and statements we cannot. For instance, if a discarnate spirit announces itself to be a French physician of the eighteenth century, we can probably discover whether such a person ever existed, and then, though with less probability, whether he can tell us anything that nobody else could possibly know, and thus his identity with the communicating spirit be established. Now it will probably be

IMMORTALITY

admitted by impartial and trained inquirers that the amount of material that comes under this heading is, in comparison with the mass of alleged communications, of very modest proportions ; so that the law of coincidence might be invoked to cover most of it. The vast amount of alleged communications we have no means of checking, because they concern what is happening in the other world. But here again certain rough tests are open to us ; and two things immediately arrest our attention : the first is the triviality of the revelations ; they tell us nothing beyond what has been communicated through purely religious revelation, save, in the main, details, not only trivial in themselves, but revealing a life almost unbelievably trivial; unless, of course, we can accept the idea that the life to come will be as trivial as this, or indeed even more so, or, that the souls normally accessible are exceedingly trivial souls. But concerning any material that transcends this triviality it again has two characteristics : it is very vague, so much so as practically to convey no information ; or what distinctive colouring it has, is generally consonant with the religious convictions of the medium, and is vaguely theosophical or vaguely Christian. Moreover, it is to be noted that a good deal of it is anti-Christian, or at least anti-Catholic, in that it definitely denies specific Catholic beliefs concerning the state of the departed ; while, more generally, it is deficient in any reference to meeting with the saints, contact with Christ, or the vision of God. This latter circumstance is bound to rouse the suspicions of Catholics, and that not because of a merely narrow exclusiveness of everything that does not coincide with their beliefs ; because, as a matter of fact, it does coincide with some of their beliefs, namely, that it would be impossible to get

IMMORTALITY

into communication with souls that were in Purgatory, while the saints in Paradise could hardly be expected to stoop to this kind of thing, and would have quite other experiences to reveal. If it were possible to think of a Limbo for souls fit neither for the heights of heaven nor for the depths of hell, with whom communication might be established, this would coincide with the affirmation of some Spiritualists that they can only get into communication with earth-bound souls. But this extension of the idea of Limbo is a precarious idea from the Catholic standpoint, while it is still more opposed to the Scholastic decision of what is possible to a discarnate soul. But from the Catholic point of view it is possible that spirits who have never been incarnate, namely devils, might gain access to the human mind. This would account for three classes of communications which mediumistic Spiritualism reports: first, the prediction of the future. There do seem to be some fairly well established cases of this, and this does seem a power which it is quite impossible to ascribe to any human mind; but it may conceivably not be beyond the mind of a fallen angel. Secondly, the mentality frequently gained contact with seems to be of at least a non-moral, or, as it has been described, a somewhat Puck-like character. But, thirdly, sometimes the communications are horribly obscene, blasphemous, and diabolical. It would only be natural that such minds should be opposed to everything Christian, and seek, though by subtle, but finally by revealing ways, to undermine faith. If this suspicion is thought to be dictated by a narrow and timid religious prejudice, yet the possibility of its truth should not be lost sight of, and for those who would try such methods as a substitute for religion, the warning should carry

IMMORTALITY

great weight, backed up as it is by the indisputable mental and moral weakening which mediumistic methods frequently involve. But in so far as our present purpose is concerned, where the evidence is either so predominantly negative or inconsistent, there is nothing here that amounts to a disproof of the truth of the Christian or Catholic view of the life of the departed. We are now left with non-mediumistic spiritualist phenomena to consider. These can practically be classed under the heading of apparitions. There is widespread and fairly convincing evidence of the appearance to their relatives or friends of those who have died, the appearances being recorded as occurring either at the very moment of death, sometimes shortly before, but much more frequently shortly after. On the cause and nature of these appearances we are left to speculation. But since the appearance is often in the condition in which the person was when dying, and as the great majority occur just after death, it does look as if it might be due to a telepathic communication of the dying person which may only register itself somewhat later in the consciousness of the recipient. The case of ghosts is slightly different; they can hardly be classed as long-delayed apparitions, but the evidence for them is very much smaller, and above all its bearing upon the condition of departed souls is confusing and ambiguous. The purely scientific investigation of psychical phenomena should of course be pursued, though methods that would injure mental and moral conditions ought to be forsworn; but it is no unfair conclusion that in all the mass of material that has now been accumulated there is certainly nothing amounting to a new revelation, there is nothing that disproves Catholic belief, and there is very little on which to build faith in the immortality of the soul.

IMMORTALITY

Nevertheless, fifty years of discussion and research have changed the general atmosphere, have at least shown what unsuspected powers are possessed by the human soul, have revealed the insatiable desire to be certain of immortality, and have thus made an approach to a reasonable faith somewhat easier. We do not propose to recount the purely philosophical arguments for immortality; for us immortality is dependent upon the existence of a personal God who loves the souls He has created. For although a few philosophers have affirmed their belief in immortality, while denying the existence of God, for most people the thought of an immortality without God would be equivalent to hell, or, at best, only a perpetuation of all that is dark, unsatisfying and meaningless in this present life. On the other hand, the consideration of what would be involved in the conclusion that the soul of man is *not* immortal is sufficient, if not to prove the contrary, at least to make it necessary to a belief in the rationality of the universe, and may perhaps for some souls be the best approach to the belief in God and the acceptance of the Christian religion. Quite apart from the difficulty of believing that our minds have emerged from a mindless world, and still retaining any belief in the validity of human thought of any kind, the contemplation of the vast process of material, physical, racial and individual evolution to produce a conscious personality which, after a life of laborious education and moral effort, must then cease to exist, presents us with a scheme as maddening as it is meaningless, and, indeed, long contemplation of it would inevitably lead to individual and racial destruction, for on every count it would make the whole of existence absolutely purposeless. Moreover, it would be in striking contradiction to the very

IMMORTALITY

doctrine of evolution itself for development to be traced through measureless time up to a mind which had only to look back upon the process and then suddenly to come to a complete end. And none of the proposed substitutes for personal immortality can relieve the situation of its irrationality and tragedy. If the human race were to continue on this earth for ever, which Science would predict to be impossible, this racial immortality would do nothing to satisfy the craving for the continuance of our personality. If our memory or even our influence lived on, we should be unconscious of that, the purpose of life would still be to seek, and there would only be borne in upon the ever more conscious and cultured mind which progress might produce the aimlessness of its personal existence. Even the emergence of a divine being as the term of cosmic development, which some modern philosophers have considered, and apparently been able to conceive, apart from its complete denial of all that man has ever understood by the idea of God, would hardly comfort the souls which contribute to His making unless in some way they revive to consciousness in Him. Even if immortality were only a day dream of man's infancy, it is a dream that is never likely to be forgotten, and must remain to shadow the brightest hopes, to cloud the clearest consciousness, and to depreciate the farthest progress man may reach, with the memory of its transcendent, delusive, but falsified vision.

But while faith in immortality seems to be reviving in our generation, even though the basis on which it is building is hardly so sure as could be wished for, yet the idea has to meet the curious objection that, as a matter of fact, the concern for immortality has proved itself inimical to human interests. Man's longing to be satisfied concerning

IMMORTALITY

the persistence of his personality beyond death has taken his eyes off the immediate concerns of daily life. In the endeavour to save his own immortal soul he has neglected the temporal condition of humanity around him. Indeed, some who are so obsessed by immortality that they see how brief is our earthly life, and how unimportant our earthly conditions, compared with the life that is eternal, have argued that it is a waste of time to strive for better conditions here on earth, for the establishment of good government or a just social order. These things matter nothing in the light of eternity. But this is a most perverse argument, at any rate for a Christian; because Christianity emphatically teaches that the character of our immortality will be determined by whether here on earth we have sought the kingdom of God, we have striven for justice, we have cared for the needs of men. Indeed, the Christian view of eternal life makes it so dependent upon life in this world that it has been the cause of frequent objection, since, it is declared, it weights this life with an intolerable burden of responsibility and gives to our brief and uncertain days a far too determining influence upon eternity. No doubt the pressure of this conception of how the life to come depends upon the life that now is has been somewhat enfeebled by the idea that faith in Christ, and at the last moment of life, may be an adequate substitute for a life spent in wickedness, or, at least, in accumulating earthly rather than heavenly treasure. But such an idea entirely overlooks the fact that faith is unreal if it is not effective in making life more unselfish, self-sacrificing and beneficial to man; and it evidently ignores the Catholic belief that between this life and its eternal reward there is set a corrective experience which must be both painful and prolonged, even if we die

IMMORTALITY

in the faith of Christ, and yet are not immediately fit for the heavenly society. It may however be objected that the fear of hell, and the belief in purgatory, which predominated before these perverted ideas of faith arose, nevertheless often conspicuously failed to restrain men from evil or to encourage them to a good life. Its inefficacy in some cases does not suffice to prove that the doctrine of immortality in its Christian interpretation has been inimical to earthly life, because it has failed to prove as beneficial as it ought to have done. While making all allowances for man's curious incapacity to let the prospect of future pleasure or pain encourage him to endure the pain or forsake the pleasure immediately before him, the relative inefficacy of his eternal prospect would be nothing compared to the effect which a complete disbelief in immortality would have upon the human race. It might conceivably not encourage vicious and violent ways, at least all at once; but there is more reason to believe that it would encourage a materialistic outlook and a restless pursuit of pleasure which in the end would have a worse effect than a recourse to vice and violence. But it is certain that its worst and most far-reaching effect would be to diminish the value of all idealism, both in attempting to secure external justice or in striving to attain interior perfection. A man would know, not only that these could have no eternal reward, but that they could have no permanent value; and seeing that the cessation of personality makes a meaningless universe, not only the value and reality, but even the sanity of all ideals would come to be questioned and at last be completely undermined.

This earthly life of ours, if it is to have any rational meaning or ethical sanction, demands faith

IMMORTALITY

in immortality, and faith in immortality demands faith in God, if immortality is not to be a mere perpetuation of earth's perplexity, and the magnification of its meaningless character on an eternal scale. And even if anyone was not convinced of immortality, or could not accept the Christian interpretation of its significance, it would perhaps be admitted that, even on the remotest possibility that both were true, it would be well to live as if they were; and further, that to live earnestly in the hope of attaining eternal life would certainly produce the noblest character and the richest type of personality, while it would relieve human life of its otherwise questionable worth and lack of meaning; and thus would do more than anything else to correct the restlessness and excesses, the contentment with evil conditions, and the perversion of evil ways, which rise ultimately from man having no sure ground, no certain aim, and no worthy attainment; which is the case if this life be all there is, and his personality, evolved through such æons, developed through such pain, and afflicted with such suffering, is nevertheless to come to an end, and not itself continue as the permanence of all it has striven to be; which is only possible if personality itself persists and there is immortality which garners and consummates the experience of earthly life.

IV

DEATH AND RESURRECTION

BETWEEN this life and the life immortal there waits for us mortals the experience called death. Death is the most certain fact in this uncertain life of ours, but despite its certainty and its universality, it is impossible for man to reconcile himself to it as to any other natural fact of life. Thus, the declaration of the Scriptures that death is not natural to man, but is due to sin, seems to find ample confirmation in the psychological effect which the anticipation of death creates. It is true that many would affirm that they have no fear of death whatsoever, but this is partly because they rarely think of it; and, indeed, those who profess themselves able to think of it calmly would, on closer examination, have to admit that, as a matter of fact, their own death remains an inconceivable thing; at any rate, when man is faced with certain death, his fear, even in the case of the strongest, is often inconcealable.

The scientific interpretation of life would, however, bid us regard death as a natural fact: according to the evolutionary hypothesis, death occurred in this world before man emerged, and is an inevitable circumstance due to man's sharing in animal life. The repulsion from death is instinctive in animals, and is to be explained as a natural device for protecting and securing the prolongation of life; and it would be held that it is only man's imagination, which enables him to anticipate death, that has

DEATH AND RESURRECTION

given to him his intensified fear of dissolution. Man's dismay at bereavement could, again, be regarded as also only an intensification of the distress which many animals show at the death of their young or their mates. Nevertheless man's self-conscious mind, with its emphasis upon individuality, and the supreme value he attaches to his personality, together with the far higher and spiritual relationships he attains with his fellows, combine to make death a psychic experience to which his mind really refuses to accommodate itself. Analysis of the human attitude towards death, moreover, makes it easy to discern that it is the sense of sin which, as St. Paul says, gives the peculiar sting to human death. It is not only the cessation of this life, with all its claims and interests, the separation from loved ones, or the violence done to conscious personality, that invest death with such unnatural significance and mental repugnance : the announcement of imminent death will frequently bring to the mind a sudden and illuminating valuation of reality, a flood of penitence at the thought of a life misspent, shame at a record so stained and spoiled, the memory of so many things done which now cannot be undone, and of so many things left undone, which must be left undone for ever. Similarly, in the case of bereavement, it will be found that where grief is inconsolable, it is often not merely the broken relationship, but the fact that the relationship has been so imperfect, which is secretly mourned. It is at any rate the fact of sin which imparts to human death its peculiar note of solemnity and sorrow; even empirically, death as man knows it and must experience it can be truthfully said to be due to sin.

It is, nevertheless, difficult to gather from Scripture or to conclude from theology what ultimate course human life was intended to take if man had not consented to sin. A perpetual life on this earth, if death had never intervened, and the decline and decay of bodily powers had been unknown, would nevertheless hardly content the soul of man; for we can hardly conceive how a communion with God could have been established under physical conditions that would have satisfied man's religious desires. We might imagine that, after an experience on earth which had enlarged his soul and given him the desire to see God face to face, man might have been translated to another sphere without anything corresponding to his present experience of death: the passage from the one realm to the other, not only accomplished without regret or fear, but without the dissolution of body and soul, the body perhaps being transformed by a natural process when the soul had reached a sufficient stage of sanctification. Even though the fall of man was foreseen, it seems necessary to hold that there was a natural possibility open to him which did not involve death as we understand it. There is therefore no inconsistency in accepting the scientific hypothesis of death as a natural and inevitable event belonging to the present order, while also believing that the present order is what it is because of sin.

The scholastic doctrine, which holds the substantial union of body and soul whose combination constitutes human personality, helps to explain why the dissolution of this union should be regarded with such horror, and should inflict such pain, not only upon the body, but upon the soul. Unlike pagan philosophy, which was tempted to regard the body as the prison-house of the soul, an unnatural confinement into which it had fallen, and a heavy hindrance to its aspirations, Christian theology not only regards the body as prepared for the dwelling of the soul, but regards the union of body and soul as necessary for the education of the soul in self-consciousness and the attainment of character. The soul owes all its knowledge to the material provided by the senses; the separation of the soul from the body therefore not only deprives the body of its animating principle, with all the pain and exhaustion this entails for the body, but it deprives the soul of its means of knowledge and its avenues of communication. The soul is therefore aghast at the prospect of mental darkness and incapacity with which death seems to threaten it. It is on these facts that a purely materialistic science has argued for the cessation of conscious life with the coming of death. The scholastic theology, accepting the same facts, acknowledges that the soul will be deprived of an organ of knowledge, and may even be bereft of self-consciousness in its separation from the body at death; but because the spirit then returns to God, it believes that for all information concerning itself and its condition it must then be dependent upon God, who will Himself impart to the soul all it needs to know. It is only because our communion with God has been so imperfect through our wilful separation from Him, our self-worship, our sin and our sensuality, that we are apt to regard such immediate dependence upon God with some degree of anxiety and distrust. In reality we have always been dependent upon God for knowledge, naturally gained or supernaturally revealed, though in the former case our pride has managed to conceal this from us. Genuine mystical experience, however, which is believed to rise above dependence upon the senses, and to come into immediate touch with God, apart from sensuous images, and by pure spiritual intuition, has already

DEATH AND RESURRECTION

tasted something of this condition of the soul in contact with God, and although this involves deprivation of the senses and darkness to the intellect, the soul is not only not afraid, but is eager for that experience to become eternal. If therefore we are to take the scholastic theory seriously, it seems to demand that when the soul is separated from the body it loses its memory, and therefore all its stores of knowledge. This paints an alarming prospect, for it would seem to involve that after death we shall not know where, what, or even who we are. It is only, however, a superficial view of things which concludes from this that we shall have lost our identity, and shall begin a purely spiritual existence in the same blank condition in which we began our earthly life. In the first place, our identity will be a fact, whether we are conscious of it or not; in the second place, the condition of the soul will consist of the moral character it has achieved, which was the exact purpose of its earthly experience. And whatever spiritual capacity for God has been attained will then be available for our vision of Him; and in Him there will be immediately discernible not only what we are, but also what God intended us to be; that is, all real knowledge of which our earthly experience has made us capable, as well as that which it will be good to know or have revealed to us. Under these purely spiritual conditions we shall therefore know ourselves better than we have known ourselves on earth; for knowledge will consist, not in a collection of facts, very imperfectly retained, or only with difficulty accessible in the storehouse of memory, nor in the arduous, obscure and precarious processes of reasoning, but in the immediate apprehension of truth, life and beauty in God; in short, in an immediate apprehension of reality, at last beyond

DEATH AND RESURRECTION

fear of mental delusion or of diminution through the medium of sense. There will be therefore immediately granted to the soul much more than earthly knowledge or mental memory could ever convey; we shall know even as we are known. All this will, however, depend upon the measure of our contact with God we have attained in this world, and upon the capacity we have developed through holy desire for Him. But our total knowledge of God will therefore, in some degree, be determined by the vision of God gained through faith while here on earth, including everything that has been learned through moral insight into Nature and the right exercise of our reason; so that this conception of the purely spiritual conditions upon which the soul must enter after death does not therefore make our earthly experience valueless, nor shall we be deprived of anything that we really possess or have gained; we shall be confronted simply with reality. Though if we have lived for shams and in pretence, if we have cared only for the pleasures of the flesh, if the higher powers of the soul, such as imagination and reason, have only been used for selfish or evil ends, then we shall certainly enter upon immortality terribly depleted, with little saved up from earth that can be converted into spiritual treasure, the seed we have sown on earth a poor harvest for the heavenly garnering.

Although the actual condition of the soul at the time of death will automatically determine its capacities for a purely spiritual life, we can believe that this will be supplemented by a revelation of God of anything further that has been prepared for us, or that it will be good for us to know. What this may be it has never entered into the mind of man to conceive, since it is beyond eye to see or ear to hear; that, however, we can trustfully leave to His will, His wisdom, and His love. This revelation will not only make up for anything of which earthly experience has unfairly deprived us, but it can now be understood how the inequalities of earthly life will be automatically redressed by the simple fact that it will not be amount of learning or subtlety of intellectual power, not to mention the accumulation of riches, the achievement of earthly fame, or the attainment of worldly power, which will determine our condition in the purely spiritual existence such as the soul will enter on after death, but simply and solely our moral character, the purity of our hearts, and our desire for holiness. These, and these only, constitute our immortal inheritance.

With these after-death conditions clearly in mind, it cannot be regarded as unnatural that religion should teach us to look upon death in such a solemn light, nor can the idea that life should consist in nothing else but a preparation for death be dismissed as a morbid perversion. Since death must be regarded as the introduction to our final and permanent state of existence, where spiritual reality alone rules, it can be replied to those who object to religious concentration on death that it is not so much death that our religion bids us prepare for as the life that follows after death; but the nature of death itself, as the moment and means of transition, must inevitably concentrate upon itself a most serious concern. The modern attitude, misunderstanding the religious concern with death, has reacted to a unquestionably morbidity equal to that from which it has felt repelled. With most people death is now never thought of, or rather the thought of it is suppressed, nevertheless only to remain in the mind, as psycho-analysis claims

DEATH AND RESURRECTION

to discover, as a pervading and sometimes paralysing fear. Moreover, when death comes in the shape of bereavement, it often proves shattering to faith, to hope, and even to reason; when its inevitable approach is announced to anyone, the very shock often hastens its arrival, and consequently every endeavour is generally made to conceal the dangerous situation, so that, if possible, the sick person may approach the very moment of death without knowing that it is imminent. The attempt is made to justify this attitude as dictated by the desire to avoid pain, or in order to give every chance of prolonging life. But if we were not all so frightened of death there would be no need for such questionable protection; anyhow, it adds little to human dignity to have to be surrounded by such a conspiracy of silence, which treats us like children, as unfit to face the facts of death as they are thought to be to learn the facts of birth; and no one can claim that such an attitude is brave or denotes a passion for facing reality. A clear and calm anticipation of death might give a saner perspective to life; for, if we could look forward upon life, as we shall certainly look backward upon it from our deathbed, it would clarify our aims, spur our efforts, and often help us to a more heroic choice. The remembrance of the inevitability, combined with the possible proximity of our own death, or that of those we love, would certainly save us from procrastinating many a kindness, and keeping back the word of apology or forgiveness. What a bequest of trouble and a heap of tangles for others to unravel we often leave behind to cloud their memory of us with reproach or bitterness; and with what heavier burden of undischarged duty and uncleared issues we come to our end for the want of a prudence which even paganism would have taught us!

DEATH AND RESURRECTION

The fact that death may come to us at any moment, in youth or old age, in health or sickness, after long warning or by sudden accident, certainly bids us to be always prepared; and serious consideration of the constant imminence of death would make it impossible for us to grow careless, or to indulge in any mood or action in which we should be ashamed to die. The uncertainty of life, therefore, should serve as a moral incentive; holy dying can adequately be prepared for only by holy living. But if it is held to be taught in the Scriptures, which the Catholic interpretation expressly emphasizes, that the advent of death sums up once for all the moral assets with which we must face eternity, does not the varying incidence of death introduce a grave disparity into the preparation which it is possible to make? The person who lives to a ripe old age is enriched by all the experience of life, has had a longer opportunity for developing virtuous character, has outgrown youthful passions and frivolities, and has more natural inclination to prepare his soul for the great change; whereas another may be cut off in infancy, with his capacities all undeveloped, or, worse still, may be snatched away by an untimely death, all unprepared, at a period when the temptations of the flesh or the vanities of this world exert their greatest attraction.

Fully to answer all the questions that are raised by the apparently accidental incidence of death must be beyond human power, until we ourselves stand on the other side of the veil, at last to comprehend the working of God's wisdom in permitting the actual conditions of earthly life, the provision which His love has made for the infinite variety of human circumstance and the inestimable value He has set upon every human soul. But the ob-

DEATH AND RESURRECTION

stinacy which Catholic thought has continually manifested against conceding a second chance, or further development beyond death, is not to be traced to any grudging spirit or narrow mentality. Catholic doctrine on this subject is due firstly to its fidelity to the most solemn warnings of Scripture, secondly to its conception of the nature of the soul and its dependence upon the body and the necessarily changeless character of eternal life, and thirdly to its realism in facing the inevitable laws of ethical consequence, undeterred by sentimentalism, and refusing to depend upon miraculous moral interventions which God's mercy might undertake, but which we have no right to rely on, as we have no revelation that sanctions such expectations. Therefore, before we abandon the Catholic belief at the dictates of what may seem like a more humane concern, or a more hopeful estimate of the life to come, it would at least be well to see whether the scholastic interpretation of the conditions of that life do not contain the real relief that the modern mind may rightly seek.

The alleged inequality in making the varying incidence of death fix the future condition of the soul rests mainly upon the point that while some die in infancy, in youth, in middle life, or before their potentialities are developed, to others there is granted the fullest opportunities that man's mortal span can embrace. Some relief to this difficulty can be found in the consideration that while there will be almost endless beatitudes of objective bliss in eternity, to which the length of earthly life can certainly contribute, there will be no difference in subjective bliss; for every soul, whether dying in infancy or in old age, will nevertheless be perfectly happy, and will actually find material for joy in the diversities of capacity for

DEATH AND RESURRECTION

bliss, since it will gain by reflection from the bliss of others an addition to its own direct mirroring of the glory of God. Moreover, it can easily be discerned that length of days does not of itself create fuller capacity for eternal life, nor is progress in sanctity always proportionate to the age we attain. Innocence of soul belongs to childhood, fervour is proper to youth, and the old adage that "those whom the gods love die young" indicates that often an early death seems to have been specially prepared for by unusual piety. On the other hand, coarsening can come with age, the dedication of adolescence can give way to the fading of high ideals, a life of sustained integrity can be marred by serious failure and wiped out by shameful collapse even in advanced years. Neither is this latter circumstance, wherein the ship, as it were, is wrecked at the harbour mouth, to be regarded as an example of how one type of injustice cancels another, for in theology, as elsewhere, two blacks do not make a white ; it is only mentioned at this point to show that brevity of life need not prevent, as longevity does not guarantee death ocurring at our highest point of moral achievement. Nor does the further complication that even an eleventh-hour repentance can create a high moral condition, owing to the opening which genuine contrition can make for the operation of grace, simply constitute a further example of a radically unjust scheme. The falling away from grace, which is theoretically possible up to the very last hour of life, is actually less likely the greater the sanctity that has been attained ; and it is an unnatural exaggeration of this likelihood which would regard anything less than grievous mortal sin as capable of any such effect. If such a final falling away occurred it would have to be regarded as already prepared for by a hidden

DEATH AND RESURRECTION

propensity which it was only wanting the occasion to reveal. On the other hand, the contrition which might open a way to Paradise at the very moment of death would have to be a very perfect contrition, and there is no moment in life in which contrition is not called for and is not possible. These considerations can be adduced to show that to allow the condition at the moment when this earthly life ends to determine the condition of the life beyond does not introduce so arbitrary an element as it might at first sight seem. We shall probably find that further light is thrown upon this issue when we come to examine the effect of the process of judgment, to which death will introduce us, and the purgation which may then be made possible. But meanwhile it must be remembered that we have been assuming, in order to face the greatest difficulties, that empirical observation concerning the apparently accidental incidence of death, and the moral condition of souls as they pass from this life, really envisages the actual situation, whereas under the Divine disposal of life and to the Divine reading of the heart things may be vastly different.

What really remains clear is sufficient to remind all men of the importance of life being continually ordered with a view to its possibly imminent end, and of every effort being made, as long as life lasts, to lay up for ourselves heavenly treasure, as Christ so earnestly exhorted us. Such remembrance need not burden life with an intolerable seriousness, invest its days with feverish striving, or demand that every possible moment shall be devoted to that contemplation in which eternal life is believed to consist. The conscious prospect of death simply emphasizes our duty of avoiding a careless outlook, an unholy life and every form of evil; that we should always be on the guard against temptation;

DEATH AND RESURRECTION

that we ought to strive to do what good we can and make the most of life's opportunities; purge our minds of all uncleanness, uncharitable thoughts and insincerities; give some time each day to self-examination, meditation, quiet recollection and simple prayer, continuing in the faith and keeping ourselves in the love of God; trusting to the performance of our religious obligations and the due reception of the sacraments to keep us faithful, aid us under temptation, inspire us to thoughts and deeds of charity, and by the very desires these observances inflame, and the sense of the values they create, direct our course through every hour of life, and by an inner transformation anticipate and prepare for all that the great change of death must bring. Common sense could hardly counsel less, a merely prudential outlook on life would demand as much, though a special vocation might call us to much more; but a truly Christian facing of the fact, and such a view of the possibilities of death can only ennoble life and enrich character. Nothing, however, can relieve death of its solemnity or evade the drastic change that it imposes: it is superficial to propose to dismiss it as a mere incident in a life of development; it is pious to accept the inevitable pain that dissolution involves as a penalty for sin, which we all have to pay, but only once; it is Christian to prepare for death by a life of love, to meet it in faith, to look beyond it in hope, and, if possible, to fortify ourselves for that final strife by a devout recourse to the help of the Last Sacraments.

It is only natural that Christian thought, regarding death as the dissolution of body and soul, a violence done to the unity of human personality due to the effect of sin, should be unable to rest content with this condition as in any sense final;

DEATH AND RESURRECTION

it must somehow be affected by that salvation proclaimed by the Christian religion, which includes the redemption of the body. This redemption, it is believed, will be accomplished by the abolition of death, the last enemy of mankind to be destroyed; but this is to be effected not by death ceasing to be the lot of mankind, at any rate so long as this present order endures, nor merely by the experience of death being alleviated by the faith in the hereafter with which it can now be met, but by a stupendous universal event which shall re-unite body and soul through the resurrection of the body, thus undoing the act which brought about their unnatural separation. Belief in the resurrection of the body is found in other religious systems, and seems to have dictated the funerary customs of primitive man; it had been adopted, though not unanimously, in the Jewish religion; but it received such an unmistakable sanction by the resurrection of Jesus Christ from the dead that it has remained a credal article of faith in the Christian religion, thus distinguishing its hope of the future life from a mere belief in the immortality of the soul.

Belief in the resurrection of the body has proved, however, prolific in creating objections, especially in modern times. It is not only that the idea of reassembling the bodies of all mankind, in so many cases long since crumbled to dust, scattered, re-incorporated in other forms, demands an almost inconceivable miracle, but the profound spirituality of the other life, as conceived by the scholastic theology, makes the reunion of body and soul seem something of an anti-climax, introducing a material element which lowers the whole conception, and intruding a carnal organism where it can surely no longer be of any use. These objections have been fostered by often unnecessarily crude conceptions of the nature of the resurrection body, however much they may have enshrined the valuable idea that the human body, which has provided a vehicle for the Incarnation, and has been made the temple of the Holy Ghost, is too sacred to be " cast as rubbish to the void." But the true conception evades this crudeness, since it is moulded more closely, not only upon the teaching of St. Paul, but upon the revelation of the nature of the risen body given to us through the resurrection of Christ. For the resurrection of Christ is proclaimed to be the firstfruits of the general resurrection; and His risen body, despite its identity with the body that was crucified and buried, was in possession of properties which made it fit to be the medium of spiritual manifestations. That body, although veritable flesh and bones, could vanish at will, pass through closed doors, and could evidently exist in a completely invisible form. It is not until recent researches into the constitution of matter that this dual form of existence, corporeally manifest and unmanifest in turn, has become conceivable; for we now know that all matter rests upon an invisible substrate, probably of the nature of pure energy, to which it could be reduced, and again be built up into tangible form, if we only knew the secret which could disintegrate the atom. This scientific fact cannot be used to explain the resurrection body of Christ, nor can it be put forward as predicting the nature of the glorified body with which the soul shall be again united, but it makes it more conceivable how there can be such a thing as a spiritual body, possessing far more wonderful powers than hitherto dreamed, no hindrance to the emancipated soul, but an instrument perfectly adapted to its manifestation, as glorious as light, even swifter in mobility, and able

DEATH AND RESURRECTION

to take any form which expresses the desire of the soul.

Even with this new light upon the possible constitution of the resurrection body, it might still be wondered why a material element should continue to have any kind of existence. We can only assume that the possession of such a medium, in addition to purely spiritual powers of communication, may add a further bliss to the heavenly life ; but there is still more satisfaction to be found in the idea that the natural order as created by God is never to be destroyed, but is to continue in a more glorified form, in which redeemed souls are to have a creative share. It may be imagined that the total energy underlying the material world will be needed to provide the bodies of resurrected humanity; and this would explain why, with a few possible exceptions, the general resurrection must be postponed until the present order has been brought to an end, while it would justify the prophecies of St. Paul, in which the redemption of the body and the deliverance of the whole creation await the revelation of the sons of God. So that the final vision is not of a world consisting only of spirit, but of the whole material order transformed in such a glorious fashion that it is fit to continue for ever, the complement and companion of the spiritual world. This view gives at least more dignity to a creation which, it is believed, issued from the hands of God, than if it were to have only a temporary existence, and ascribes to the will of its Creator a permanent purpose surely more in accordance with what we must conceive to be the working of the Divine mind.

V

JUDGMENT

IT is a doctrine of Catholic theology, it has hitherto been the belief of almost every type of Christian thought, and, indeed, it has been a common article of almost every religious system whatsoever, that after death man will have to face a process of judgment, in which he will receive the reward of whatever good and the punishment of whatever evil he has done in this life. How this process is set in operation, and what standards of good and evil are to be applied have naturally been differently conceived. In the Christian religion, under the influence of the Scriptures, this process has been represented as a kind of general assize, in which all human souls are summoned before the throne of God, the records of every man's life are consulted, and his destiny apportioned upon the merit or demerit, the faith or unfaith, they reveal. The obvious symbolism of this picture has nevertheless proved somewhat of a stumbling-block to those who believe they have reached a more spiritual conception of ethical processes, and the consequences that they automatically register in the condition of the soul. There is a wide disposition to-day to believe in a process of judgment which is present, continuous and immanent, every act and thought of the soul not only being infallibly recorded in the unconscious mind, but unchangeably colouring the ethical constitution, and therefore inevitably determining the

JUDGMENT

ultimate destiny of the soul. Every soul in every moment of its career is shaping its ultimate direction; all the forces that play upon it, and all the choices that are made, must in the end be embodied in a resultant force and an unalterable direction, dictated by the dominant desire, and dictating the final destiny of the soul, thus determining its eternal condition and carrying it by a natural attraction to its own place, that place being fixed, not by some arbitrary decree, but by a kind of spiritual gravitation, the interior condition of the soul determining the effect which its spiritual environment must have upon it, and therefore producing beatitude or misery. This process, however, it is felt, must be already ceaselessly at work here in this present world and should not be regarded as postponed until after death or as needing to be inaugurated by any kind of personal arbitration, however exalted or divine. The Scriptures themselves could be appealed to in support of this conception; the Fourth Gospel in particular constantly refers to a judgment which is not included in Christ's purpose and does not depend upon His will, for He expressly declares that He did not come into the world to judge the world, but judgment had been automatically inaugurated by His coming, since light having come into the world, men would adjust themselves to it according to their preference for light or their love of darkness, and thus judge themselves. Therefore what is believed to be strictly ethical and entirely spiritual thought concludes that the dreadful pictures of the General Judgment in which all humanity will be summoned before the Great White Throne are only symbols of what really is an automatic, uninterrupted and wholly interior, process.

JUDGMENT

But when it is remembered that death involves the dissolution of the intimate union of body and soul, it might, even by this type of thought, be conceded that death itself must constitute a crisis in this process of judgment, since it makes an end to that kind of experience which comes to us through earthly life, the physical world and our bodily senses, and leaves us to face nothing save the purely spiritual harvest we have gathered from our experience of life. But this type of thought tends to be so idealistic, that it does not take the dependence of the soul upon the body very seriously, and thus is inclined to believe that life beyond death goes on much the same, save perhaps for the accumulation of fresh experiences and the opportunity for further development. That death itself inaugurates or needs to be supplemented by judgment is therefore admitted with difficulty. Yet surely the general instinct of humanity, which has expected some judgment after death, is governed by a profounder thought and a more serious estimate of the significance of death. And if the pictures of the General Judgment are interpreted as symbolical, as they undoubtedly must be; for the records on which judgment is pronounced obviously do not need to be books with carefully kept accounts, since they are written both in the soul of man and in the mind of God; yet the symbolism is not to be interpreted as representing a merely automatic or wholly interior process. It is surely reasonable for the mind to demand that what is obscure in this life of ours shall be made manifest, and that not only the destiny of our own soul, but that of all others, shall not merely be disclosed, but shall be morally approved by all. Most of us are unaware of the significance of our daily acts and the tendency of our thoughts; if we look at life externally, and even if we watch closely the development of other souls, so much remains not only hidden, but appears fortuitous, precarious or unjust. But when we subject our own souls to the closest scrutiny, and adopt the most spiritual valuation, some of our most earnest efforts seem only to bring forth defeat, while some of our highest attainments seem to be accidental or reached without effort. Every inquiring mind, and every believer in ethical justice and spiritual reality, must crave at least a revelation of the compensating rewards or merited deserts, even if the actual process of judgment is immanent and continuous. We desire to see how the laws of life work out, and how they conform with absolute justice, and for that some confirming and consummating process seems necessary. We desire to see how everything is motived by absolute justice, a creative purpose and a final end which shall justify the power and life which the Creator has brought into existence. We want to see this world of ours with its multitude of souls, so differing in their original endowments and varying opportunities, illuminated by the operation of a sublime and compassionate mercy overspreading all His works and a wonderful and ever to be praised wisdom threading through all His ways. A general judgment, therefore, bringing home to every soul the justice and mercy of God, a final clearing up of all difficulties and obscurities, the apportioning of a destiny which all souls must approve, and especially those to whom it is appointed, must take place if the mind of man and his passion for justice are to be fully satisfied. Such a judgment must take place beyond this life, and at the end of human history on this earth; and whereas the literal picture of a judg-

JUDGMENT

ment seat, the gathering before it of all souls and the opening of the books which contain the secrets of all heart outstrips the practical imagination as to how it could be accomplished, it is entirely satisfying to the spiritual understanding, if it is recognized to be the symbol of a revelation which shall be made to all souls at the last that the judgments of God are just. Indeed, it is only a literal mind or an impoverished spiritual valuation which will not rejoice in this symbolism, recognizing that it alone can convey to us, with the present limitations of our minds, the full assurance of a final clearing up of all things, the justification of existence and justice for every soul.

The inevitable postponement of the General Judgment to the end of time and the climax of human history, and since it must be preceded by the General Resurrection, in which the deeds done in the body shall have some corresponding registration in the body that then shall be reunited to the soul, creates a gap between death and the Judgment, for all save those who die just before the end of the world, of vast and perplexing extent. For it seems to have been the idea of some of the early Fathers, temporarily revived by some of the Reformers, that the souls of the departed must remain in an unconscious condition until the General Resurrection takes place; the Scriptural declaration that they are " asleep in Jesus " being taken literally; and if the scholastic theory is accepted that the separation of the soul from the body deprives it of the ordinary avenues of knowledge, of the storehouse of memory and of its organ of consciousness, then this would seem to be the inevitable conclusion. It is only natural, however, that Christian thought could not long remain content with the idea that all the departed must remain in an unconscious state until the General Resurrection and the Final Judgment. The recollection that if departed souls remained thus unconscious, what to us is a great lapse of time would be as nothing to them, even when ameliorated by the Reformation assumption that the state of those souls is not sheer unconsciousness, but one of blissful repose, and even felicity, fails to satisfy the Christian instinct. "To be asleep *in* Jesus" surely cannot mean the same as being "asleep *to* Jesus." How could the soul that has here enjoyed communion with God be in felicity, if it were less conscious of God than while in this life? The conception of what has been called the Intermediate State, however lightened by various ascriptions to it of peace and felicity, has now almost everywhere broken down. In the Early Church it had to give way before the growing belief that, first, the martyrs, and then those who had reached sanctity by other means, had been admitted to the vision of God, which the practice of the invocation of saints obviously demanded. By the fourteenth century it had become the agreed doctrine of the Church that all souls, on departing this life, entered upon their eternal destiny, though, if that destiny were eternal bliss, some more or less lengthy preparation for it might be necessary. But such beliefs, including Reformation thought, which eventually came to believe that those who died in faith immediately entered heaven, were difficult to reconcile with the postponement of all judgment until the Last Day. Catholic thought has solved the problem by the assumption that there is a judgment for every soul to be gone through immediately after death, distinguished from the General Judgment in being private, whereas that will be public, and since it concerns

JUDGMENT

only the individual soul, denominated " the Particular Judgment."

It is strange that there should, however, have been any hesitation in working towards this doctrine, since, on turning back to the Scriptures, we find there ample support for it. Our Lord's parable of the Rich Man and Lazarus depicts the souls of these two men as already having entered upon some degree of their reward or punishment; even if Abraham's bosom is not actually heaven, or the Hades in which the rich man found himself not the same as hell. Similarly, the answer to the penitent thief that he should be in Paradise with Christ that very day, promises some measure of immediate bliss, if indeed it does not promise entrance to supreme bliss; for which we should have to posit such a perfect contrition that any further preparation would be rendered unnecessary, and an immediate entrance granted into heaven itself. In the apocalyptic vision granted to St. John the souls of the martyrs are already under the altar of God: those who have come out of great tribulation have already passed beyond all sorrow and are being led by Christ to fountains of living water; and heroic souls are already enrolled in the armies which follow the Lamb and make war upon the armies of the Beast. Now if some souls have already reached a condition of supreme felicity, some kind of judgment must have taken place; and we have the statement in the Epistle to the Hebrews, " It is appointed unto men once to die, and after this, judgment," which certainly conveys an impression that there is at least no great lapse of time between the two. The working out of this doctrine of the Particular Judgment occurring immediately after death is an interesting example of how scattered sayings of Scripture are only illumined by centuries of thought; and, moreover, of how they often depend, as research shows, on an assumed background of thought, as in this case, even going back to Jewish belief that some souls immediately pass into a state of conscious blessedness at death; while the full reconciliation, significance and necessary implications are only recognized, brought out and fitted together by the finally defined doctrine of the Church.

The defined doctrine of the Particular Judgment nevertheless leaves a good deal to be explored which has not been decided; but with the aid of hints in the Scripture, in accordance with the principles of scholastic theology, and following up a well-defined tendency of thought among Catholic thinkers, we may move towards a view of the Particular Judgment which is spiritually illuminating, and also does full justice to the element of truth underlying the modern preference for an automatic judgment. It is stated in Scripture that all judgment has been committed to the Son of man, and that it is before the judgment seat of Christ that we must all appear. Now first it should be noted that the judgment has been committed to Christ because He is the Son of man; for that emphasizes not only the fact that our judgment will be in the hands of one who has understood our life by actual experience from within, and therefore will be of the most merciful and compassionate kind, but it is a judgment which has been set in operation by His becoming Son of man; it is therefore a judgment bound up with the Incarnation, because it confronts mankind with the image in which it was created. Secondly, there is a hint in the Apocalypse that the only form visible on the throne of God will be a Lamb as it had been slain, while there is the explicit statement that

JUDGMENT

"every eye shall see Him, and they which pierced Him." Therefore the belief has grown up amongst some Catholic theologians, surely of great value and truth, that the Particular Judgment will be inaugurated for the soul by the vision of Christ as Incarnate and Crucified. When it is remembered that, according to the scholastic theology, the soul immediately after death will have no knowledge save that which God Himself is pleased to bestow, and be in possession of not even the memory of its life on earth, but only of its actual moral condition, then it can be understood how, when the soul is confronted with the incarnate and crucified Christ, a process of judgment will be inaugurated that must work out for every soul with perfect fairness. In the first place, surely we are entitled to believe that those souls who, while on earth, have known nothing of Christ and His cross, because they have dwelt beyond the area of Gospel light, as well as those souls who, though they have heard, have never really seen or understood what the Incarnation and the Crucifixion meant for them, will be presented with a full revelation of the love of God as set forth in Christ's humanity and Christ's cross. Without something like this it seems impossible to reconcile the inevitable limitation of the Gospel, first, to the area of its proclamation, and then to its individual understanding, with the purpose of God and man's need of salvation. In the second place, such a revelation will not mean some overwhelming manifestation which will deprive the soul of moral choice; it will not be a vision of God in His glory or in His Essence, such as it is believed must for ever unite the soul to God, but of Christ in His humanity and of Christ as crucified. It therefore will present every soul with precisely that test of faith with which Christ confronted those He came

JUDGMENT

in contact with in His earthly life and who witnessed His crucifixion, further illuminated perhaps with a revelation equal to that granted to His disciples both during His life and after His Resurrection, as to who He was, and why He died. All souls shall have an opportunity of knowing that the incarnate Christ is God seeking them, and they shall discern in the Cross the assurance of His love and forgiveness. This will not provide anything in the nature of what is called a "second chance," which Christian thought has generally rejected; for millions of souls it will be the *first chance*. Moreover, while it will contain a blessed revelation, and perhaps a much-needed assurance of the reality, personality, love and forgiveness of God, the response that any soul may make to this will be already prepared for by what its attitude has been in this life to all that is good, true and beautiful. Thus it will be a confirmation and a reward of what may be called implicit faith. On the other hand, those who have lived in the full light of the Christian Gospel, and even those to whom there has come the great gift of faith, will have to face a judgment that contains in it an equal test. A merely theological knowledge of the Incarnation, a merely conventional assent to the Atonement wrought by Christ, a faith that has not been expressed in life, will carry no knowledge or effect past death, and will leave us confronted, not with that vision of God which unites us to Him, but only with a vision of Christ in His crucified humanity. This will test the soul in the same way as men were tested who met with Christ in the flesh, and on the same basis as the heathen are tested after death. If there has been anything in our worship that has been unreal and hypocritical, if we have failed to discern in the meekness of Christ the wisdom of God, and in

JUDGMENT

Christ's consent to the Cross the power of God, the mere knowledge we have gained will not prevent us from then rejecting Christ, any more than it prevented some of the Jews, who saw Him in the flesh, and heard His teaching, from consenting to His crucifixion. At the Particular Judgment a conventional acceptance of Christianity will put us in no better position than that of a pagan. It is therefore a judgment that will redress what has been merely accidental in the light that has visited us and in the revelation of which we have received knowledge here in this life; while, on the other hand, every genuine welcome of truth, desire for beauty and struggle after good will prove a preparation that will help us to face the test. That this will be the character of this judgment is borne out by that most searching and most disquieting picture of the Judgment which Christ gave us in the Parable of the Shepherd dividing the Sheep from the Goats. From that parable it is obvious that some who have had no means of recognizing Christ, but nevertheless have served the least of His brethren by acts of justice and mercy, will receive the same reward as if they had consciously served Him; whereas others who have known Him, but have failed to discern Him as expecting to be served in those who were in need, will be rejected as unknown by Him. The Particular Judgment will therefore satisfy those purely ethical conditions which some modern minds have demanded as the only true basis of judgment, while, at the same time, bringing a revelation that will make known to souls the personal source and eternal reality of the good they have loved and served, even though they have lived in ignorance of God, or have been unable to attain to faith in His goodness or hope of the life to come. The confronting of every soul

JUDGMENT

with Christ in the Particular Judgment will have just that effect, provide just that test and determine just that decision, to which the proclamation of the Christian Gospel is meant to bring souls here and now in this world; not with the purpose of bringing about their condemnation, as Christ Himself was careful to disown, but for the purpose of effecting their full salvation; though with the inevitable consequence of condemnation, if, when the nature of salvation is seen and the condition of its offer is understood, men deliberately reject it. But if the soul is to be confronted not only with Christ as incarnate, but with Christ as crucified, there is another element in the judgment, both of test and of assurance, that still needs to be considered.

If it is true that when we depart out of this life we shall carry hence no memory of it, but only the moral disposition that we have gained, it seems to follow that we shall not even retain the memory of our sins; and from every ethical and spiritual consideration it seems necessary that we should face our sins in the light of eternity, not only in order to know the basis of our judgment, but, where sin has been due to failure and has not been carried to the extent of final and absolute rebellion, in order to overcome the effect of such sin; for while such sin is not mortal sin, in that it does not consist in the soul turning absolutely away from its Creator, it is venial sin, and has therefore weakened the soul, lessened its capacity for God and misdirected its disposition. Our own judgment of our sins in this life is lamentably imperfect; the things that we are most inclined to mourn, and that cause us the deepest pain, are often not the things which are of the greatest danger to the soul. Even an accurate memory of our sins would therefore be a very imperfect

JUDGMENT

ground for any judgment. If we are to enter into any kind of higher life where truth alone prevails and spiritual vision dominates, we must get a true view of our sin and truly repent of it. For this we must depend upon a revelation of some kind, the impartation by God of such knowledge as is necessary for us, which will more than make up for the inadequacy of earthly knowledge and the inaccuracy of human memory. Our own memory of our sins, as they have affected our conscience and left a mark upon our minds, would be an entirely insufficient preparation for the spiritual valuation and capacity on which the bliss of heaven depends; therefore a deeper process of judgment than our own conscience has provided must be inaugurated, and it is precisely this that the vision of Christ crucified will present to every soul. We shall be confronted with our sins, not merely as they have hurt others, not merely as they have harmed ourselves, but as they have been registered upon the perfect conscience of our Lord, and engraved themselves upon His crucified humanity. We shall have to contemplate the wounds of the crucifixion in order both to understand and feel what sin was to Him and what it has done to Him. And only if we are willing to bear the pain which that must involve, as well as to accept the forgiveness of which His willingness to bear that pain assures us, can we pass the test that will admit us to whatever purgation is necessary and whatever degree of bliss is thereafter open to us.

There is therefore contained in the Particular Judgment that which gives to every Christian and compassionate soul a sufficiently wide hope for all mankind; not only the hope of a perfectly just, but of a supremely merciful judgment; while at the same time it warns the soul of an

JUDGMENT

inevitable test before which nothing but the willingness to be utterly sincere and humble will be able to stand. The more Christian any soul is, the more will it anticipate being confronted with Christ after death with mingled fear and confidence, driving it to seek the only adequate preparation for that test in a sincerity that desires to face ethical realities as they are and in the quickening of all spiritual aspiration, all its hopes based on the faith that works by love. Indeed, such a soul will know that nothing less than being crucified with Christ, entering into the fellowship of His suffering for sin and living a life of self-sacrifice, can prepare for the Particular Judgment in such a way as shall enable the soul to stand before the Son of Man, and pass to the further vision of God, safely, swiftly, and without deprivation. We all have to face the claim of love and the disclosure of sin, and face it in the revelation of One who is both our Judge and our Saviour, our Lord and our Friend. It will be the embodiment of a test of sincerity; it will be a bestowal of that reward which we have the capacity to embrace; it will effect the clearing away of the last shadow of obscurity or wavering of indecision, and will confirm the soul for ever along the line of its highest desire. It is in the operation of this Particular Judgment that there lie our hopes for others whose understanding has been so obscure and whose faith has been so unfulfilled; while for ourselves it inculcates that fear of the Lord which is the beginning of wisdom, a fear that can only be cast out when perfect love has been gained and confirmed with eternal life. Into what immediate condition this judgment will then usher our souls we shall have to consider when we come to the question of Purgatory, and only

JUDGMENT

a little more needs to be said concerning the still remaining necessity for a general judgment, even after the operation of the Particular Judgment has taken place.

The General Judgment will not reverse, or in any way alter the Particular Judgment; it will only make universal the secret operation of the Particular Judgment; so that all souls will be satisfied, both concerning themselves and others. If this involves the revelation of the secrets of all hearts, and therefore even of the sins of those who have already enjoyed the bliss of heaven, it may be felt that this will involve a revival of pain and a further torment of shame; but it must be considered that we shall then so love truth that we shall have ceased to fear it; and moreover there will be disclosed, along with the basis of each soul's judgment, the revelation of the forgiveness of God, and our own contrite acceptance of it; so that any pain arising from this publication of our sins will be wiped out by the joy of forgiveness, and the recalling of our sins will only call forth the more ecstatic praise of Him who loved us and loosed us from them through His sacrifice for our salvation. But all will then know why some souls who had been judged in this world to be unworthy of the name of Christian bear it there in high glory, while others who made it their boast have been denied by Christ before His Father in heaven. The General Judgment shall leave not one wrong unrighted, not one falsehood unexposed, not one good unrewarded, not one evil uncondemned, not one difficulty or doubt uncleared. The inner working of God's laws will be revealed to all; the redemptive value of all pain will be traced out; all the tears and blood that have been shed will be shown in their cleansing operation

JUDGMENT

as they are brought into relationship to the tears of Christ's heart and the blood of His Passion. The apparent injustices of earth shall have their compensations revealed, and its real injustices shall be more than redressed. Faith shall then be shown to be, not the obscure, uncertain and arbitrary thing it often appears to our observation, but that fundamental choice by which the soul is justified, because by it there is given to every soul what it really desires: to those who desire the highest, the reward which will fill them with humble joy; while unfaith shall be seen to be the desire of the lowest, its reward only what was desired, and the condemnation it entails acknowledged, even by those who are condemned, as absolutely just. The Final Judgment will be the justification of God and His purposes, and therefore the consolation of all who have believed in goodness and have striven for the highest.

VI

PURGATORY

IT could be claimed that it was over the question of Purgatory that the Reformation took its rise, for it was Tetzel's sale of Indulgences that fired the train of revolt in Luther's mind and caused the storm of indignation to burst forth which had long been gathering, with such profound consequences for subsequent history. Yet, strangely enough, it is at the point of this very same doctrine that the Reformation Movement is now exhibiting a tendency to return to the Catholic faith. Whether the belief that as the money dropped into his bag souls were released from Purgatory was an actual statement of Tetzel or only a popular misunderstanding of something he said, there is no doubt that there had gathered round the idea of Purgatory many superstitions which did not belong to the essence of the doctrine. Many of these were discouraged by the Tridentine definition, which contents itself with the modest declaration that Purgatory exists, while deprecating the introduction of over-subtle discussions on the subject. No doubt this decision was meant to clear the ground of a vast mass of unauthorized speculation, and simply to maintain as essential doctrine that there is a place or condition of temporal punishment for those who depart this life in grace, and yet are not entirely free from venial faults, or who have not fully paid the satisfaction due for their transgressions. Even about this reduced doctrine there clings a certain difficulty for minds not accustomed to Catholic terminology, because it seems to

PURGATORY

presuppose a certain arbitrary imposition of punishment and to involve ideas of payment and satisfaction alien to spiritual conditions and divine demands. On the other hand, modern religious thought is impressed with the need of some preparatory purgation for most souls passing from this world, before they can be considered fit for the direct vision, the overwhelming glory and the immediate presence of God which constitute Heaven. Nevertheless, a considerable advance has to be made both in the further interpretation of Catholic doctrine and in a deeper appreciation by modern thought before any real acceptance of the doctrine of Purgatory can be looked for. In some modern thought there is a tendency to welcome the doctrine of Purgatory because it hopes or believes that spiritual progress will continue beyond this world. It not only feels that most souls when they leave this life are not deserving of Hell, but it is inclined to believe that no soul can ever be in that condition; a question which we shall have to examine when we come to consider the Catholic doctrine of Hell. On the other hand, while it feels that few souls are really fit for Heaven, it is also inclined to regard the traditional conception of Heaven as inadequate, or at least one with which most souls could never be content without considerable preliminary training, since it is supposed to consist mainly in the contemplation of God. It is a curious nemesis of intellectual rebellion which, overthrowing the authority of the Church's teaching, began by rejecting the idea of any intermediate purgatorial state between that of Heaven and Hell, and now seems likely to end by believing neither in Heaven nor Hell, but only in Purgatory, if Purgatory can only be interpreted as a condition of gradual, perpetual and inevitable progress.

PURGATORY

It needs to be made clear at the outset that the Catholic doctrine by no means corresponds to this modern notion. In the first place, Purgatory is only for those who depart this life in a state of grace, to whom, however, certain imperfections attach which have to be removed. Secondly, Purgatory is regarded as a place of severe pain; indeed, the pain of a purging fire, though in this state it is not laid down that the fire need be considered as of a material kind; in distinction, therefore, from the prevailing Catholic doctrine concerning the fire of Hell. Thirdly, the purgatorial process is by no means regarded as equivalent to a state of progress, Catholic doctrine remaining firmly wedded to the idea that as the soul leaves this world so it remains to all eternity, with no further possibility of enlargement or growth in its spiritual capacity. Nevertheless, the apparent deadlock between inquiring thought and Catholic definition need not be pressed at this stage to sheer opposition. There is a more generous interpretation possible on the Catholic side, and a more spiritual understanding to be sought for in the genuine religious thought of our generation that still remains unable to accept the teaching of the Catholic Church. And it is to that task of reconciliation that we can address ourselves with some hope, because of the wide scope left for exploring and applying what is involved in Catholic doctrine, and because of the breakdown of prejudice and the approximation to real spiritual standards of judgment in the modern mind. It is only by a profoundly personal conception of religion, thoroughly enlightened as to the centrality of Christ and the necessity of His Atonement, that we shall find any point of real reconciliation. On the one side we must seek a spiritual interpretation of the doctrinal terminology of satisfaction and payment,

PURGATORY

of pain and punishment, which does not readily commend itself to the mind impressed with the spiritual and ethical issues involved. But it must be remembered that Christ Himself employed exactly such terminology when He spoke of a soul being delivered to the tormentors till it should pay all that was due, or of those servants who at their lord's coming will have to be beaten with many stripes or with few, according to their knowledge of their lord's will. It is obvious that we have to translate this symbolism of payment and pain out of the realm of the financial or physical into that of ethical and spiritual reality. On the other side, however, the modern mind needs to abandon, as on further examination it is bound to do, its too easy notions of a progress determined by the mere sequence of time, of an enlargement of the soul conceived as an immanent development, independent of any further light coming to it from without, and of a redemptive process which is self-originated and automatic, and therefore able to dispense with the redemption wrought by divine grace, the work of Christ and the activity of the Holy Spirit. With such an interpretation on the one side, and such deeper understanding on the other, the spiritual rationality, nay, the beauty and mercy, as well as the necessity of a purgatorial process, can be sufficiently demonstrated.

But a further hindrance to the acceptance of the doctrine has to be removed from the path of those Christians who, standing by the sufficiency of Scripture, maintain that there is no room in its revelation of the other life for any kind of Purgatory. The type of Protestant who regards the Scriptures as providing a full doctrinal system without need of interpretation or further guidance is, from one cause or another, steadily disappearing. Most

PURGATORY

enlightened Bible students would admit that the Scriptures, by their very nature, were not intended to define, or can be expected even to mention, all the doctrines necessary to the Christian faith. There is a wide background assumed; there was a tradition of teaching and worship preceding the very beginning of the New Testament writings and growing up while they were in composition. Many Protestants would now be willing to admit that the Christian faith was not founded on documents and is not exhausted by Scriptural declarations, but is assumed by them and is only partly reflected therein. On the other hand, the Catholic, while recognizing an authority in the Scriptures which Protestants are now everywhere relinquishing, not only looks to theology to deduce, and to the authority of the Church to define, the ever-growing realization of the original revelation, but maintains that the germ of Catholic doctrine can always be found in the Scriptures, and that nothing inconsistent with the general sense of Scripture can ever be put forward by the Church as doctrine necessary to be believed. Therefore the Catholic defence of the idea of Purgatory undertakes to show that sufficient hints and assumptions are found in the New Testament to warrant the tradition and to sanction developments of the doctrine.

Our Lord spoke of some sins which can be forgiven neither in this world nor in the next; which clearly implies that some sins can be forgiven in the other world that are not forgiven here. He also speaks of penalties inflicted upon His servants for unfaithfulness, heavier where His known will has been transgressed, lighter where His will had not been known. In the Epistle to the Hebrews the heavenly Jerusalem is said to contain "the spirits of just men made perfect;" and here it seems necessary to

PURGATORY

assume that the process of perfection is something additional to the righteousness they had achieved, and that this process takes place subsequent to earthly life; for while we can become righteous here on earth, it would be admitted that few attain to perfection. The Apostle Paul speaks of the Day which shall reveal the character of a man's work, because it will be proved by fire; and here a process seems to be indicated that shall destroy in a man's work all that is impermanent and useless, leaving behind only that which can abide. As a result of this ordeal, the Apostle says, a man may suffer great loss, though he himself will be saved, " yet so as through fire." Here obviously a fire is at work which does not touch the real things of the soul, but does consume all else, and is a necessary process if the man himself is to be saved. In this reference a complete and indisputable doctrine of purgation seems to be involved.

It is a little doubtful whether either Purgatory or Hell is involved in Christ's parable of the rich man and Lazarus: the rich man is said to be in Hades, which is not necessarily Hell, and yet he is in torment; Lazarus is in Abraham's bosom, which is hardly to be identified with Heaven. What gives some hope that the rich man is not in eternal Hell is, first, that he has some vision of the souls who are in peace; and, secondly, that he has some concern for the brethren he has left behind in this world, which seems to indicate some change in his character. No doubt this parable assumes ordinary Jewish thought on the subject of the after-life, without necessarily endorsing it; and although the common interpretation is that Lazarus was in Heaven and the rich man in Hell, nevertheless the reference to Abraham's bosom rather than to Paradise fits in with the Church's doctrine that until Christ's Ascen-

PURGATORY

sion not even the souls of the Patriarchs had entered Paradise; while the declaration in answer to the rich man's request that there was a great gulf fixed between him and Lazarus, which could not be crossed from either side, would be equally true concerning the Church's doctrine of the Limbo of the Patriarchs and of the condition of souls in Purgatory. Whether this parable should be so used to sanction the doctrine of Purgatory or not, it is clear that there is not only room but a demand for it to be found in the Scriptures.

Catholic doctrine on the subject cannot rest content merely with the hints found in Scripture, nor does the Tridentine definition forbid us to go beyond its assertion that there is merely such a place as Purgatory. Without entering upon the subtle and disturbing speculations that the Tridentine decrees deprecate, there have been unreproved Catholic contributions to the subject true to spiritual principles and full of illumination and comfort. At the same time, we have to put aside popular conceptions of Purgatory which still seem to prevail among the less thoughtful of the Catholic population and even of the priesthood, and which partly account for the Protestant misconceptions and suspicions. Under these conceptions Purgatory is conceived as almost exactly like Hell, consisting of the same fiery punishment, save that it is of a temporary character, its duration partly determined by the satisfaction that has to be made for sins imperfectly repented of, or by the reparation that even the best repentance must include, and partly by the prayers and sacrifices made on behalf of the souls in Purgatory by those on earth interested in their welfare. These are conceptions which must necessarily appear crude in a brief statement, but they are not only capable of, they demand fertiliza-

PURGATORY

tion by more spiritual ideas and detailed explanation. For this purpose we can turn to two poetical conceptions, not to be appealed to as if they were on the level of defined doctrine, but which have never been condemned and are obviously of great spiritual value. The first of them is Dante's "Purgatorio," which can be accepted as a spiritualization of the general teaching on the subject in the Middle Ages. As students of that poem will have discerned, the essence of Purgatory is there set out as a condition of profound penitence : primarily, souls are there conceived as intensely contrite for their sin, feeling its sinfulness as they never did on earth ; secondarily, they are represented as making reparation for their sin by practising with strenuous diligence the contrary virtue. If this can all be conceived, as Dante certainly meant that it should be, as a mystical process, in which sin is now seen for what it is, and is so hated, while virtue is so loved that the soul becomes finally detached from the one and attached to the other, the need and the value of such a purgation can be understood and accepted by all spiritually alert minds. Especially has Dante left to us one noble phrase when Virgil promises him that he shall see souls "content in the fire," which lets in a flood of light on the purgatorial notion, namely, that it is not the infliction of pain involuntarily borne, but whatever the nature of the pain be, it is actually welcomed because of its purgatorial character ; and there can be only one kind of pain that has that effect : the pain of penitence. The other poem, perhaps even more familiar, is that of Newman's "Dream of Gerontius." There the voluntary character of the pain endured is again stressed, but its cause is traced not so much to penitence for sin as to the fact that the soul has seen Christ Incarnate and has been so filled with

PURGATORY

the desire to live for ever with Him, yet is so filled with shame at its unworthiness, that it welcomes some temporary hiding of His face until the soul is made capable of living with the pure light which flows from His glorious Presence. The many relevant lines of that poem cannot here be repeated, and it would spoil their beauty to paraphrase them, but the doctrine that inspires them is this : that it is when the soul sees Christ that it knows perfectly, for the first time, what sin is and what holiness is ; and for very longing after that holiness and for desire to be with Christ it is willing to undergo whatever pain of purgation is necessary to make it possible to dwell for ever close to His heart. Here is a doctrine which conveys to all understanding souls the truth that the infinitely holy God would prove a consuming fire to every soul that dared to approach Him ; while, nevertheless, there is an inextinguishable desire in every soul touched by grace to see God in His beauty and actually to partake of His holiness. Therefore if that blessed consummation is ever to be reached, perfect holiness must become the very essence of the soul ; nothing can produce in us that essence but perfect charity, which must include not only the love of what God is, but the hatred of all that is contrary. The vision of Christ, which we have every reason to assume the soul will be confronted with when it passes from this life, is therefore to reveal the nature of our sin; not so much because of the awakening of a perfect remembrance of all we have done, or the stirring of a more perfect conscience on the subject than we had developed in our earthly life, but because we now see ourselves in contrast with the perfect revelation of Christ's sinless Humanity, and our sins in the passion they occasioned Him ; for we shall see Him not only as Incarnate, but as

PURGATORY

Crucified Love. The conflict of passionate desire for holiness and intense hatred of sin, into which this vision will plunge us, is seen to be inevitable, and supremely necessary for the perfect purging of the soul from all attachment to sin; for no one can but love Christ and hate sin who has looked upon His sacred wounds. Nevertheless, it still remains a little difficult to conceive what this process of penitence involves, or can actually achieve. The idea of a purgatorial fire is of obvious symbolic value, but if we are going to understand what the fire is that can purge the soul, we shall have to undertake a further inquiry into its spiritual meaning and ethical effect.

Catholic theology can fortunately direct us to an illuminating work on this subject which promises to give us what we are seeking, namely, the treatise on " Purgatory " written by St. Catherine of Genoa. Without attempting an exposition of this work, which is quite short and accessible to all, we shall content ourselves with drawing attention to some of its more important propositions. The first is somewhat startling, for the writer discountenances any idea that Purgatory is caused by the remembrance of our sins. The only place she leaves for that is in some experience antecedent to Purgatory; it is only in the passage from this life, and then for once only, that souls behold the cause for which they are in Purgatory, and never again do they consider it. To understand what this means we have again to bring in the idea that the soul sees Christ immediately after death; and it is the love of Him then awakened that constitutes Purgatory, because it is a love to which the whole nature, because of its imperfections, is unable all at once to attain. The object, therefore, of Purgatory is not so much to attain a perfect contrition for sin as to attain that

PURGATORY

perfect charity which alone makes the soul capable of dwelling with Love. This doctrine, therefore, emphasizes the positive rather than the negative side of the purgatorial process. A second point to be noticed is that St. Catherine insists that Purgatory consists both of an intense pain, like the pain of Hell, for it is a pain of limitless intensity, and yet also of an intense joy; and the two feelings exist side by side. This is possible because the pain really consists in the beatific instinct being debarred from complete fruition. In short, the pain is due to nothing else but the longing for God on the one side, and, on the other, whatever in the soul hinders that longing from immediate fulfilment. There is in this doctrine a sufficient acknowledgement of the popular idea of the pain of Purgatory, but with the interpretation that it is nothing else but the pain of intensified love. There is also a sufficient recognition of the popular idea that one would wish to be in Purgatory as short a time as possible, while it is balanced by the Saint's declaration that souls in Purgatory have no other will but to be in that place, because they know that so long as they are there, they need to be there, and so long as they need to be there, they desire to be nowhere else. Moreover, although they are temporarily shut out from the actual vision of God, there is an understanding between God and the soul, ever growing more intense, until the soul is ready to see Him and be united to Him. As will be recognized, the Saint utilizes the still popular ideas, but invests them all with a profounder spiritual meaning. But the third point to be noticed is perhaps the most illuminating of all, and is contained in an illustration which helps to give us a better conception of Purgatory than any number of merely doctrinal statements. St. Catherine likens the nature of the soul

PURGATORY

to gold whose surface was meant to reflect the glory of God, and sin to the presence in it of alloy and the accumulation upon it of rust; and the action of the presence of God upon the soul is like the action of fire upon gold; it burns away the alloy and destroys the rust, and thus makes the gold so pure that the fire can exercise no further action upon it, and all the rust being destroyed, it then reflects the glory of God as if it were burnished.

This illustration, apart from the attraction of its natural beauty, presents a most illuminating conception of Purgatory, for it shows that what determines the soul's stay in Purgatory is simply its actual condition and its ability to endure the glory of God. When there is nothing more for the fire to destroy in the soul, then there is no more pain, and the moment all the alloy is purged, then the soul, being now like pure gold, only rejoices in the flames which once caused it pain. This conveys the idea that Purgatory is not simply a place of banishment from the Presence of God, arbitrarily imposed as a punishment; Purgatory is nothing but the Presence of God as it affects the impure soul; for the glory of God, to which the soul is introduced, so long as the soul retains the slightest lack of love or trace of sin, first of all blinds it with its light, and secondly scorches it with its holy flame; but as the rust and alloy of sin are purged away the soul is able to look upon God and to rejoice in His presence; that is to say, the fires of Purgatory are nothing else than the glory of God, the darkness of separation and the pain which the soul suffers being simply due to the sensation that the glory of God produces upon the soul that has in it the slightest attachment to sin or the least imperfection of charity. This illustration has the advantage of conveying the conception

PURGATORY

of a spiritual condition rather than of spatial separation, of an ethical change rather than of an inflicted penalty, remitted when sufficient has been paid. That glory of God in which the Seraphim burn with joy must be, to the soul stained with sin, purgatorial. The soul does not escape from Purgatory, strictly speaking, by changing its place; but the flame of God's glory, which is destructive of everything connected with sin, and is intolerable save to perfect love, becomes the food, the life, the joy of the soul, when once sin is perfectly purged away and the soul is filled with nothing but the pure love of God.

Purgatory is therefore an inevitable prelude to any close contact with God such as the soul desires and Heaven consists in, if with this desire there remains any conflicting attachment or unworthy motive. But it is this desire rather than simply the fact of being a sinner which brings the soul under the purgatorial process. Purgatory would not purge away sin where there was no desire for God; the soul would never come into contact with its fires unless it longed for the glory of God. Therefore Purgatory cannot be counted upon as a process available in order to make all sinners fit for Heaven: it is only for those who die in grace and faith; that is, for those who, when they see Christ, have the grace which comes from faith confirmed, or whose response to universal grace is thus awakened to saving faith. Purgatory is not available for those who die impenitent in their sin; for, in this case, the motive which plunges the soul into Purgatory would be lacking, namely, the love of God and desire to dwell in His Presence.

Neither, again, is Purgatory to be regarded as a Catholic sanction for the modern belief in progress beyond this life. That conception will call for

PURGATORY

further examination when we come to consider Heaven; but the processes of Purgatory do not produce anything that can strictly be described as progress. Its processes only remove from the soul hindrances to the realization of its full capacity; but its capacity is already determined by its condition, its character, and its desire when it leaves this world. The effect of Purgatory is therefore negative rather than positive. It, as it were, removes the rust from the coin: it does not increase its face value; it burns out the alloy: it does not increase the amount of gold; it polishes the mirror: it does not enlarge its reflective area.

Therefore we must not look to Purgatory to do something for us which this life cannot, and thus diminish our efforts after holiness, or postpone repentance with the assurance that Purgatory will make up for all deficiencies acquiesced in and defects allowed to remain. To postpone anything for Purgatory to accomplish would be to run the risk of never attaining to it at all. On the other hand, the aim of the soul should be not merely to shorten the duration of Purgatory, but to escape it altogether. For although the most saintly will doubt their fitness for the immediate Presence of God, it ought to be remembered that it is not advanced holiness which is necessary to evade Purgatory, since Purgatory will not increase any attainment, but a perfect repentance for sin and a perfect love of God up to the level of our own conscience and knowledge. It might be conceivable that a soul destined for a very high place in glory would have to endure a considerable time in Purgatory, whereas a soul which was only fit for a lower place in glory might pass through Purgatory sooner, or know nothing of Purgatory at all. If the Paradise promised immediately to the penitent thief signifies

PURGATORY

Heaven, his case would be an illustration of this possibility: he saw Christ crucified, and assuming that he was moved to perfect contrition and charity at the sight, this is the condition which Purgatory is designed to produce; so that, if he had attained that condition, he was ready for Paradise, however lowly a place he might be granted there. Indeed, a soul that has in this life been granted great light, but who has not perfectly responded to it, may need the purgatorial process more than one with lower light who has been faithful to it, though the former may eventually mount higher in the heavenly glory. Purgatory is therefore not so much for sinners, as such, as for saints; for although it is for the cleansing from the stains of sin, it effects this through love, and only through pain so far as that is an effect of love.

Sometimes it is piously hoped that one's purgatory may have been endured on earth, because of the suffering that has had to be borne; but this can only be rightly hoped for if the suffering has had a definitely purgatorial effect: nothing can be expected from earthly suffering merely inflicted or endured; for, as we have seen, the suffering of Purgatory is incidental; it is the desire for perfect love that is the real cause of its purifying process. Profound contrition and perfect aspiration after holiness, purely for the sake of the love of God, form the safest anticipation of Purgatory, for when desire to be with Christ and love of God's glory are intense, the purging flame would be so welcome that it would have little to destroy and would strike upon the soul rather with the effect of gladdening light and generous sunshine.

Such considerations may perhaps without temerity be entertained within the area of defined doctrine, and they may perhaps do something to remove from the doctrine the superstitions and unworthy fears that have obscured its beauty and spirituality, while they make it impossible to charge against the doctrine the idea of a mechanical reparation or the substitution of human merit in place of the sole sufficiency of Christ's sacrifice and the cleansing power of His blood, which Protestants of one type or another have sometimes condemned the doctrine for involving. It is the looking upon Christ Crucified with the eye of faith which makes man just, in Purgatory as on earth ; the possibility of acquiring merit is definitely denied to souls in Purgatory by St. Catherine : the merit there available is not ours, but Christ's ; for it is His purity and passion that wake in the holy souls cleansing contrition and the fire of divine charity.

VII

HEAVEN

HEAVEN is the eternal reward of faith, the consummation of salvation, the goal of God's purpose for humanity, the bliss prepared from all eternity for the created soul, even as the soul was created in order to enjoy that bliss; so that it might well be expected that Christian theology should have much to say on this subject, and that the doctrine of Heaven should be clear, full and rich. Yet it is here that theology seems to lose its power; not because there is nothing to be said, but that nothing can be said that is adequate to the subject. Theology is compelled at this point to hand over its task to the symbolism of poetry or the mysticism of prayer. Hell has always been easier to describe than Heaven, and although the appeal to the penalty of Hell and the reward of Heaven has come under condemnation, as confusing the motive by which we should turn from evil and seek the good, and while the pains of Hell can be made sufficiently terrifying and have often been exaggerated and overpressed, it cannot really be said that Heaven has ever been made a false motive for faith or goodness, for it is quite impossible to make its delights attractive, save to those who in some degree have already tasted of them. So here theology must be content with hints that will seem vague and statements that must seem cold. It is therefore strange to find modern secular thought complaining about the Christian concern with Heaven because it unfairly competes with temporal concerns, the glory of Heaven casting a shadow upon earthly beauty, and its eternal endurance depreciating the significance of time; with the result that some people have despised this life and have sighed for the life to come, while others have been content with unjust and uncomfortable earthly conditions in the belief that Heaven would more than redress them; since, in view of eternal life, it hardly seemed worth while concerning themselves with anything so short and impermanent as earthly life. If the expectation of Heaven really ever had any such effect upon the estimate of earth, which is to be doubted, it certainly has so no longer; for now the complaint is that the traditional picture of Heaven has no attraction, and would only prove to be intolerably tedious. On the other hand, modern religious thought is inclined to demand that Heaven must be the ultimate guaranteed goal of every soul that has been created, or if it is not, then that the creation of man ought never to have been undertaken, for surely there can be no content with man or satisfaction with God unless every soul is at last brought to the heavenly condition. Yet, on further reflection, modern thought is inclined to fly to the other extreme, and maintain that Heaven is psychologically impossible. The human soul can never attain to a condition in which it is either for ever safe or completely satisfied: if it is going to be absolutely safe, it must mean that its freedom has been destroyed; if it is going to be entirely satisfied, it means that its progress has come to an end. Thus some have turned to seek satisfaction for the highest aspirations of the soul in a Heaven in which there must be not only perpetual progress, but constant striving, and therefore the continual danger of a further fall. So that while a previous

HEAVEN

generation was inclined to doubt the existence of Hell, the present generation is inclined to doubt the possibility of Heaven ; if Hell was thought to be inconsistent with the goodness of God, the goodness of man is now thought to be incapable of Heaven.

The failure of the conventional picture of Heaven to attract the modern mind is due, in the first place, to its inevitably symbolic character. The Gospels tell us very little about heavenly conditions ; it is only in the Book of Revelation that we get detailed descriptions of the Heavenly City, but these, when literally interpreted, seem to be lacking in beauty, while the life they depict seems to lack variety. This is due to a mistaken understanding of the peculiar symbolism of that book, which throughout employs a symbolism of idea which will not bear translation into artistic representation. Any endeavour to represent in form or colour the seer's description of the Holy City would produce a picture not only unattractive, but impossible and ridiculous. The symbolism used is meant to be translated solely by the spiritual imagination. For instance, the golden streets, the gates of pearl and the walls of precious stones are only meant to indicate the nature of the heavenly valuation. What men have striven on earth to possess themselves of and hoard in secret is there used for the humblest purposes and is possessed in common, the idea being to indicate that Heaven so surpasses anything earth can bestow that earth's highest is Heaven's lowest. Again, the occupation in a continuous worship may have suggested to some minds an unending series of Church services, which, even at their best performance and with the highest spiritual appreciations, would soon weary ; while the ceaseless repetition of anthems might prove tedious to the unmusical and torture to the musical. The actuality of which these things are the symbol is not easily imaginable, for they indicate that the soul is confronted with such a vision of reality that all its powers are absorbed in adoring worship, while the soul is in such a condition of ecstasy that it has no expression but that of song, and no language but that of praise; and since the soul's condition is unchangeable, this experience and its expression must be eternal.

When there is added to this description of Heaven's bliss the exacting conditions which would exclude any soul with the slightest taint of sin, or the mind with any thought that could defile, a demand not only for purity of motive, but for actual perfection of nature, even to the holiest this might seem beyond the possibility of human attainment, and, to the secular-minded, would seem to impose conditions that would only be repressive, monotonous and uninteresting. It is not, of course, realized by those who cling to sin in any form or degree that these conditions are essential to subjective happiness and social harmony, and that they are a necessary protection of Heaven's unclouded joy and the guarantee of a beatitude that can have no diminution or end. Christian imagination has tried to fill out this picture with something more attractive to the ordinary mind, and in poetry and hymnody has endeavoured to describe the superb beauty, the serene light of the heavenly land and the heavenly atmosphere, painting Heaven as a paradise, like a beautiful park, where nature and art have conspired to produce perfection, and where all that makes earth's pastoral joys imperfect, storm and rain, cold and heat, cloud and mist, are unknown. Others have concentrated more upon the happy human relationships, the restoration of sundered

HEAVEN

friendships, the renewal of the love that death has broken; for much of the modern interest in the other world is centred upon these things, to the neglect of the vision of God and the communion of the soul with Him. Heaven will certainly provide perfect social relationships, but a very little thought will show that these cannot be its chief, or primary, basis. Human relationships on earth have not only been imperfect; they have often been burdensome and intolerable, and a good many people would almost look for a Heaven where they could get away from some people whom they never wish to meet again.

The Christian view of Heaven is therefore rightly dominated by the idea that it is a place created by the immediate and unveiled presence of God, that it is a condition which the vision of Him produces in the soul, and that all other things are secondary; and although they are not to be forgotten or dismissed as unessential to human bliss, what makes them an augmentation of that bliss is the fact that Heaven is the place where God is all in all. Therefore, unless the soul is awakened to desire God, and that desire has become so dominant that its satisfaction is the one thing that is hoped for and aimed at; unless the soul has already in some degree found its happiness in God, or at least knows that its happiness will be found in Him and nowhere else; and unless the soul has at least a passion for that purity without which God cannot be seen, and for that holiness without which no soul could dwell for a moment in His presence, the idea of Heaven cannot be made intelligible, not to say attractive. Indeed, it has to be pointed out that if the soul retains the slightest attachment to sin, if its love of God is imperfect, Heaven would prove quite intolerable; in fact, would be much

HEAVEN

more like Hell. The soul unprepared for God, without some pure desire for Him, unless its happiness were already centred in Him, would find God's presence a source of embarrassment; it would feel anything but at home in Heaven; it would find itself in conditions that it could not endure, and where it could not be happy for a moment. Hence the absolute psychological necessity not only of Heaven being prepared for the blessed, but of the blessed being prepared for Heaven; and therefore the necessity of the demand for faith in this life, and even for Purgatory beyond, if the Heaven of God's dwelling-place is to be also the dwelling-place of the human soul.

It seems only like an additional difficulty and a further burden when we turn from the symbolic delights and the social joys of Heaven which, in other ages at any rate, and probably still for some to-day, have proved a source of attraction, to consider the terms of reality into which the scholastic theology would translate this symbolism, and the secondary place to which it would relegate a good deal of the popular conception of Heaven. According to the Scholastic Theology the bliss of Heaven consists in the contemplation of God; and this contemplation, it declares, consists in the intellectual vision of God; that is to say, in the immediate intuition of the essence of God by the human mind, seeing God as He actually is. While this involves something quite different from the idea of God comprehended by the intellect, something much more direct and immediate, namely, the actual contact of the human mind with the mind of God; and while it is something just as real as, and yet utterly superior to, physical vision of any material form, it is nevertheless utterly impossible to represent to our minds in their present condition

HEAVEN

what the contemplation of God actually is. Catholic Theology believes that the symbolic expression "face to face" means nothing less than seeing God as He is; nevertheless, since what God actually is surpasses anything we can imagine or conceive, this declaration still leaves us without any possible conception of what Heaven consists in, unless we happen to have advanced so far in the state of mystical prayer that some faint foreshadowing of the beatific vision has been already granted to us. That same theology goes on, however, to assure us that, however inconceivable at present the direct contemplation of God may be, it will bring absolute, final and thrilling satisfaction to the soul. We shall not only behold, we shall enjoy God; and this enjoyment will be so great that its only limitation will be the utmost capacities of the soul when elevated by grace within and glory without. It is this surpassing and unchangeable joy which shall draw out every faculty of the soul in adoring worship, and shall produce such joy as can only be expressed in ecstatic and endless thanksgiving that God is, that He is what He is, that God has created us for Himself, and has at last permitted us to gaze upon His glory.

It is the pure act of contemplation which constitutes the supreme bliss of Heaven; but the very effort to assure us of its attraction brings with it certain difficulties. In the first place, we cannot imagine anything so perfect that nothing more perfect is desired or could exist; while the attainment of such a perfection carries with it the negative corollary that it is unchangeable, and therefore the act of contemplation becomes literally a single act, simple, absorbing and unchanging. This explanation seems to rule out the idea of progress and the possibility of paying attention to anything

HEAVEN

but God. We have previously had to refer to this conception, so contrary to modern ideas, that the life beyond contains no possibility of progress when once Heaven is reached. This conception is dictated by the fact that progress involves change, and if we are to change from one state to another, then the state we are in at any moment will be one of imperfection, and to be aware of that would awaken the pain of unsatisfied desire. Then, again, change needs and creates time, which brings back the fear of tedium. Now Heaven has no place for anything but the perfect, and it belongs to eternity. This conception probably strikes a chill upon many minds to whom continual change and perpetual activity seem to be the essential conditions of happiness; but it can be replied that while Heaven consists in the vision of God, it must be remembered that God is the All in all; that is, He is in all things and in all men, and all things will be seen in Him. We shall see not only God in His essence, but the mind of God in relation to His creation; it means, therefore, seeing the purpose of God for His world and for every individual soul. Therefore, although our gaze is concentrated upon God, we see all else in Him, and although only in Him, because in Him, only as perfect and in harmony. There is therefore not only room for the beauty of the created world and the multitude of individual souls, and both in their essence and perfection, but we are definitely assured that we shall see not only the Trinity in unity, but the Humanity of Christ in the Godhead. It must seem to our minds, under the present conditions of time, that this is a vision which it will not only take eternity for us to grasp, but even though everything can be seen in God, it will have to be seen in detail, as well as in the glorious unity that in Him it attains,

HEAVEN

and therefore the eye of the soul will have to range from one thing to another; indeed, unless this is possible, we shall not feel assured against the possibility of absorption or tedium. The Scholastic Theology is, however, more anxious that we shall conceive Heaven as based upon union with God, and therefore being a participation in His eternity, than to concede to our restless minds and our experience of the necessity of change any real movement or any actual progress. It reminds us that to the mind of God there is no past, present, or future. His mind beholds everything in one " eternal now "; that His nature is absolutely unchangeable because it is perfect, and it is in that nature that we are to participate; and since it is God's nature that is blessed, it is in His eternal and unchanging nature that our bliss will consist.

It is necessary for the philosophical or the spiritually advanced to have this assurance of the eternal changelessness of heavenly contemplation, otherwise eternity would seem to be nothing more than a long-drawn-out extension of time, the experience of which would prove only tedious and fail to satisfy the real desires of the soul. It must therefore be maintained that the condition of the heavenly life is not characterized by extension of time, but by intensity of experience; that eternity is not just time multiplied; it is a condition from which time is entirely absent. On the other hand, the Scholastic Theology is prepared to make some concessions to human frailty and to allow us to believe in some movement of the mind, as it were from one delight to another; in the possession of a power to distinguish within God the temporal creation and individual souls, and yet to maintain that this movement is not the deepest thing, and everything else is only secondary to God: the profoundest activity of Heaven and its deepest bliss will be the one pure act of the mind absorbing all the faculties in concentration upon God. It is the instantaneous yet eternal character of that glance, and the infinite perfection of its object, that will make our bliss perfect, unclouded by even the shadow of any further desire, and therefore guaranteed against the peril of restlessness or loss. The contemplation of God in His essence is supreme bliss, not only because of the satisfying joy of the vision, but because this contemplation produces in us, first, a likeness to God, so that we rejoice in what God rejoices in, and so our bliss is found in that which is identical with His own; but, secondly, there is an actual union of our nature with God which Catholic theologians do not hesitate to describe as deification. This does not mean that our individuality is absorbed in God, neither does it mean that we become divine in any other than a secondary, corporate and dependent sense, yet no lesser word is sufficient to describe the actual participation in the nature of God; and it is this which brings to our frail and finite souls a satisfaction not only past imagination or desire, but also past any danger either of defection or satiety. Thus the heavenly vision of God is called the beatific vision because it creates and for ever fixes the soul in a condition of bliss; so that once this vision is attained there can be no recurrence of temptation or fear of a further fall. The heart is fixed, the will becomes one with the will of God, and sin is as impossible to the beatified soul as to God Himself. This does not mean the loss, but rather the gain, of freedom. The happy symbolism of the ever-open gates of Heaven is meant to convey the assurance that there is no kind of repression in Heaven; everyone does as he likes, but everyone likes

HEAVEN

but one and the same thing, God and what God loves.

Heaven therefore contains the sole guarantee of the satisfaction of the human soul, which, despite its own finitude, is dissatisfied with anything less than the infinite. There is a real perfection which every soul can and will attain, and that perfection will be such that it will never be visited by the pain of unsatisfied desire; it will never know anything that mars, spoils, or makes defective. This attainment of perfection does not, however, entail the idea that all souls will be equal in the glory in which they are clothed, or that all souls will be equal in their capacity for God: these will differ in individual souls according to the faith and the attainment gained upon earth, yet every soul will be satisfied to the utmost of its capacity; and although it will be able to discern the greater glory in others, it will only rejoice in it, not only because it is the will of God, which is perfect, but it will receive something from the souls which have greater capacity than itself. Each soul will not only see God according to its capcity, but it will also reflect the glory of God, and therefore magnify that glory beyond what any soul could of itself see or receive. It is this which explains the necessity not only for communion with God, but for the continuation of the communion of the saints.

This conception of Heaven, to which Christian theology leads us, needs now to be defended against two objections. The first is one that appears to take a very high line, for it maintains that it only corrupts the motive of loving the good and following the true if these things are rewarded in Heaven: men are bound to look to the reward rather than to seek the virtue for itself. But, in the first place, it must be pointed out how spiritual the reward of Heaven is; it is nothing more than being endowed with the sum of all virtues, namely likeness to God. There have no doubt been popular conceptions of the heavenly reward which concentrated more upon the symbolic representations or the secondary bliss of Heaven, and some of the saints have been so jealous of any possible corruption of the motive of seeking God that they have maintained that God must be sought for Himself alone and not for His gifts. It is impossible, however, to press this distinction too far; we must frankly recognize that there never can be a complete obliteration of self-interest in seeking God, since He is not only our highest aim, He is also our chief good. Moreover, the distinction is one that really cannot be made, for the satisfaction of the soul, which comes from the vision of God and union with Him, is absolutely unattainable if God is desired merely as a personal satisfaction, apart from love for His character and consent to His purposes. In God existence and essence are one; that He is, and what He is are the same thing; we cannot love Him unless we love goodness, and we cannot rest in the Holy One unless we are holy too. Supreme personality and infinite ethical principle are united in Him, and both must be sought together if He is to be our everlasting joy and our final satisfaction. It is surely a matter for thankfulness and trust that our highest aims and our deepest desires meet in eternity and are both satisfied in God.

The other objection is of an opposite kind. It is that Heaven and the conditions of the heavenly life demand too much from man, and must therefore exclude all but an infinitesimal fraction of humanity, composed of the rarest souls, who alone could breathe the air of Heaven and endure the burning light of God's glory. The fact that there are degrees

HEAVEN

of glory in Heaven somewhat diminishes this difficulty, but the fact that the conditions are exacting for all, needs to be faced. It is, first of all, quite obvious that faith is essential to the attainment of the heavenly realm : we must walk by faith on earth if we would attain to the vision of Heaven, and this because faith exercises those very faculties which will enable us to see God. For, as we have seen, on the one hand, God cannot be seen by mortal eye, and, on the other, He must be apprehended more immediately than as a mere idea in the mind. This obviously demands the wakening and training of faculties to which alone the glory of God is rendered visible. Therefore it is only possible to open the kingdom of Heaven to believers ; it can be for the faithful alone. We shall have to discuss more fully later on the nature of saving faith and what it is that actually determines the destiny of the soul, but it is sufficient to state at this point that the faith which opens Heaven to the soul can be nothing arbitrary or accidental, still less can it be a bare and unfruitful faith, a mere believing that God is, or believing something about Him, as, for instance, that He is One ; it must be a faith which has a double effect, in that it leads to the love of God and in that it creates purity of heart. Without the love of God, the capacity for seeing God which faith creates would nevertheless be destroyed at the sight of Him ; only the love of His glory could stand those blinding rays and burning fires. The coming and working of faith are mysterious enough, but unless faith has this effect it is not faith, and, further, whatever has this effect is faith. To those who truly and sincerely love God Heaven is open. That purity of heart and holiness are also demanded might seem discouraging even to the most saintly ; for purity of heart seems to demand

HEAVEN

a nature spotless to the core, stainless even to the eyes of God who looks upon the heart; while surely holiness is an attainment of the very highest order. It is difficult to put the matter so that it will embrace at once the humble fear of the saint that he is not good enough for Heaven, and the desire to make Heaven accessible for the lowliest and humblest. But "pure in heart" may be taken to describe not so much those who are pure through and through, but those whose intentions, desires and aspirations are pure; therefore those who perhaps have not actually been able to achieve the purity they desire, but whose desire is pure and passionate. Holiness, again, may exist only in germ on earth, and be brought to perfection only through Purgatory; for while it needs at least pure desire if we are to see God, it is the vision of God and that alone that will make us like Him. But to enable us to keep together the maximum demand and the minimum necessity which heavenly conditions call for, we must have recourse to the mercy and grace of God. No human soul, however saintly its attainment, will owe its entrance into the heavenly kingdom to anything which can be traced solely to its own efforts: Heaven is possible for any soul only if God have mercy upon it and if He supply it with the necessary grace; and we know that He would have mercy upon all men, and that He withholds His grace from none. Therefore there is hope even for those of very low attainment who yet have real aspiration and sincere love.

For the particular place that any soul comes to occupy in glory, and for the capacity for God that has been created by earthly experience, we have to look to that anticipation of Heaven in which prayer consists, and to that service of man which is the fruit of love. It is in mystical prayer that

HEAVEN

we find it possible to understand, in some degree, even now, how the contemplation of God banishes time and satisfies desire, so utterly is the mind absorbed and does the soul rejoice in the perfect activity of contemplation. Yet we know that mystical gifts and ecstasies are not in themselves a guarantee of some high place in glory, or even of reaching Heaven at all. It is the depth of the desire to which prayer has given expression, and not necessarily the degree of satisfaction attained, that prepares the soul for Heaven; and this may be felt by the pure and simple.

While no amount of good works are in themselves sufficient to open Heaven to any soul, the good works that are prompted by faith, and done for the love of God, must make a real difference to the degree of enjoyment in Heaven; and it is this that governs the addition of secondary bliss secured by the communion of saints. All service to our fellows which has really served them, that, for instance, in which we have made the love of God real to them, must have the effect of increasing the joy and widening the circle of the heavenly society to which we shall gain admission. The conditions which govern our contacts and relationships with other souls in Heaven are not determined by spatial contiguity or physical sight, but by spiritual affinity: and souls that we have helped will be attached to us by special bonds of gratitude and love. Here is a heavenly incentive to the cultivation of real fellowship, high friendship and pure love on earth. The law which determines that if we do not love our neighbour whom we have seen, we cannot love God whom we have not seen, not only means that here on earth our love of God must express itself in love of neighbour, but that in the heavenly life we shall have to depend con-

HEAVEN

siderably upon our apprehension of God's glory for the reflection of Him which we shall see in other souls with whom we have a spiritual affinity, or with whom we have formed true spiritual relationships.

The exhortation to make our calling and election sure, to win for ourselves an abundant entrance into the kingdom of God, cannot depend on making the picture of Heaven seductive, or so depict its joys that they shall corrupt the motive by which Heaven is sought; for those joys are beyond description or even imagination. Nevertheless it is Heaven that the soul of man was created to enjoy, and it is Heaven alone which can satisfy man's soul. Theology can do nothing more than declare that such satisfaction is possible, and indicate that which alone can supremely and everlastingly satisfy; what that satisfaction is it must leave the soul itself to discover, in some dim anticipation here, in full experience only there.

VIII

HELL

THE doctrine of Hell has proved the point at which, for many, especially in the last generation, the whole system of Christian thought has seemed to break down. For it has appeared to many serious and susceptible minds that if God could create such a place of suffering, torture and misery, and send anyone there; or even if in some sense Hell is self-created and is the inevitable consequence of certain tendencies of character; then it is not only impossible to believe in the omnipotence of God, it is impossible to believe in His love or even in His wisdom. It may be, however, that it is not so much the doctrine of Hell, in its Scriptural sense and Catholic definition, that has occasioned its rejection, but the false conceptions which have gathered about it, the exaggeration of its tortures, and especially the acquiescence, and apparently even the satisfaction, of some in the idea that Hell is the destiny of the majority of the human race.

But even if we endeavour to relieve the doctrine of every exaggeration of punishment, or the multiplication of the numbers who, on any theological sanction, are bound to go to Hell, we are still faced with a doctrine that contains serious difficulties, and from which the natural man, for many reasons, recoils. It is obviously dangerous to minimize the punishments of Hell or to encourage any soul to take risks; for the words of our Lord Himself are of such a character that almost nothing can add to their dreadfulness, and His warnings are

HELL

specifically addressed to any who might be tempted to complacency. Moreover, if we question the doctrine, we find ourselves at once entangled in speculations, which, although doubtless motived by zeal for the love of God and charity towards mankind, have, nevertheless, involved the rejection of Scripture, the questioning of Christ's teaching, as well as the proposing of alternative doctrines unknown to revelation and contrary to reason.

In the first place, many attempts have been made to get rid of the idea of Hell altogether, by regarding it as a false conception due to taking metaphorical passages in the Scriptures too literally. But while metaphor on this subject is frequent, and must be allowed for, and while many references occur in parables where details cannot be pressed into doctrine at all, the reality the metaphors represent cannot well be less dreadful, or the warnings embodied in parables need any the less be heeded when they are translated into guidance for practical life. Some idea of a place of punishment for the wicked can be found in nearly all pagan religions, and the fear of falling into some such conditions as Hell is believed to contain, has always haunted the mind of man. This is, however, no reason in itself for rejecting the idea: on the contrary; and little evidence can be produced to show either that the pure teaching of Christ has been interpolated in this interest, or that His mind was falsely coloured on this point by the harsh judgments and cruel ideas of His age. The idea of Hell is too constantly found and firmly intertwined in the recorded teaching of Christ for any valid criticism to sanction its excision; and with our Lord's belief in the Father's love, and with His immense solicitude for the soul of man, for Him to have given such teaching and employed such

HELL

descriptions only adds to their weight and demands the more careful consideration. That the doctrine of Hell should be met with throughout the New Testament, and be so firmly and uncompromisingly embedded in the Church's defined faith, may not impress some minds; but it would at least be wise first of all to accept the idea, and try to understand its meaning and necessity, before we adopt the far-reaching alternatives of wholesale rejection and speculative reconstruction.

Taking advantage of expressions which seem to imply that Hell is simply a synonym for the destruction of body and soul, the doctrine of Annihilation has been preferred by some as the real meaning of the New Testament teaching about Hell. But this interpretation has not only been rejected by the Catholic Church, it cannot seriously be maintained by an informed, exact and impartial examination of the relevant Scriptural material. No doubt He who created the soul could annihilate it; but to do so would involve a withdrawal of God's gift of existence essential to the individual soul, and would create a change in His mind and purpose unthinkable of the Divine nature.

In all the passages in the New Testament which appear to speak of the destruction both of body and soul, or the death of the soul, it can easily be discerned that these never describe the complete annihilation of personality, but simply the destruction of the harmony and happiness man was intended to attain, or the missing of that ideal existence for which the soul was intended, and compared with which any other existence is called death. The death of the soul no more means the ending of existence than does the death of the body. Moreover Annihilationism has included many differing conceptions. With some forms of the idea it has meant a gradual, and with others an immediate destruction after death; and these slip down to the conception of conditional immortality in which Hell simply stands for the non-attainment of any existence beyond this life. To propose, as the doctrine of conditional immortality does, that man's soul is not naturally immortal, that the eternal life which is the result of faith in Christ is the only form of existence that continues beyond the grave, that man is not so much immortal as immortable, is not only false to the general conception of the Scriptures, but denies a practically universal instinct of the human mind, passionately defended by the highest thought and logical acumen of rational philosophy. It would have the effect of dividing the human race into two distinct species; as intolerable to Christian judgment as it is to natural science.

Others have put forward the suggestion that Hell is remedial and therefore temporary; that after souls have there suffered the due reward for their sins they will have learned from their suffering, they will repent of their sin and thus be able to be admitted to Heaven. This theory simply substitutes the idea of Purgatory for that of Hell, which not only confuses the whole Catholic scheme, while adopting one of its hitherto rejected points, but of course overlooks the traditional doctrine that Purgatory is only for those who have faith and die in grace. The eternity of Hell is not only clearly stated in the New Testament, but it is stated in exactly the same language as the eternity of Heaven, and any doubt cast upon the one would cast the same doubt upon the other. To proclaim the eternity of either as a place, while denying this eternity as a condition, would be an empty affirmation, and, on any spiritual interpretation of the life to come, a meaningless distinction. Origen, the

HELL

only one of the early Fathers who toyed with the idea of Hell as a possibly temporary condition, was driven by his own logic to believe that the heavenly condition must be equally impermanent: if souls could repent in eternity, then the souls of the blessed must be equally capable of change, and therefore might be tempted and so be capable of a further fall. There are certainly texts in the New Testament which speak of the restoration of all things, of Death and of Hell being themselves destroyed, of the triumphal reign of Christ, and of God being all in all; but while they may give some ground for the hope that everything has not been revealed to us concerning the eternal realm, and that God's purposes have not been exhausted by what we know at present of the power and extent of His salvation; what has been revealed, and what has been clearly stated, prohibit us from building anything upon such statements which would enable anyone to teach with authority the final salvation of impenitent human souls, or even, as some have done, the reclamation of the devil and the fallen angels. A dogmatic universalism, the theory that all souls must be saved, is not only beyond anything that the New Testament sanctions, it has to ignore or even rescind the freedom of the human will. We may wish that all souls should be saved, for we know that God does more, He wills it; but He wills it on condition that each soul also wills it. We can both hope for all and pray for anyone that the love of God may win the consent of their will, but we cannot proclaim on the authority of the New Testament, the traditional teaching of the Church, or even the conclusion of human reason that it is impossible to conceive of any soul being finally and eternally lost. It is difficult to understand the heart that does not wish all souls to be

HELL

saved; but it is equally difficult to understand the mind that can proclaim all souls *will* be saved. For if we turn altogether from revelation, and simply observe human habits, watch earthly careers and even examine the mind of man with all the resources of modern psychology, we shall find little to confirm the idea that Hell is merely the creation of the theological mind, or the notion of its permanence due to our failure to allow for the resources of the Divine Love. So great is the place given by Catholic theology to human freedom that it is believed that until the will is fixed for ever by the vision of God, there can never be any certainty that man will not fall away and turn to evil. It is believed that that vision leaves to those who receive it no choice but to unite themselves to God by an unalterable act of will. That act no more deprives man of freedom than God is deprived of freedom, who nevertheless cannot sin; but that vision destroys all desire for anything but God; he who has thus seen God can will nothing else. The question might, however, then be raised why God does not grant to all men that vision which would seal their souls to love of the good, in adoration of God and in permanent union with Him. The answer is, in the first place, that men cannot be granted that vision unless their will has been previously won to the purposes of God through their vision of Christ in His crucified humanity; God will not destroy human freedom in order to fix the will to good. And, in the second place, if a soul still attracted to wickedness, entangled in self-love, or with any conflicting desire, could see God as He is, that vision would only cause agonizing suffering, if it did not bring about its instant destruction. Only the soul that has been sufficiently prepared by faith and love, or purged by cleansing fires from the slightest

HELL

imperfection, could for a moment endure the vision of God. Therefore to introduce to Heaven any soul unfitted for its conditions would make Heaven to that soul seem even worse than Hell. Moreover, all psychology teaches us that the habits of man's mind tend to fixation; character moves inevitably towards final good or evil. The deliberate rejection of truth tends to beget an attitude towards truth which makes it distasteful to the mind, and deprives the truth of its power to appeal; just because it is true it stands no chance with such a mind. Moreover, it is sometimes seen that the mind will plunge itself into a gloom from which it refuses to be set free, because it has come to prefer misery to happiness; it will wrap itself round with a despair that is irrational, and torture itself with things that do not really exist. There are few who have had wide and intimate contact with souls who will not have met those who, in this world, have already made a hell for themselves, not only in their external conditions, but in their own minds, and who will fight to the death against anything that would deliver them from the conditions they have created, or save their minds from the thoughts that torture them. It is not a question of God creating Hell, of sending souls there, or of inflicting eternal torture upon them: Hell is a condition that man can bring upon himself; and on purely rational and psychological grounds Hell seems more conceivable than Heaven. If man is to reach Heaven he must be lifted there by supernatural power, and he will have to be prepared for it by supernatural grace. His natural tendency seems to be rather to make a hell of this world, and if he fails in that, to make a hell of his own mind. Therefore rational considerations and psychological observations can do nothing to relieve Christian doctrine of the possibility of a hell for the human soul. Nothing but revelation could establish the impossibility or impermanence of Hell, and no such revelation exists.

It is, however, not only natural, but a Christian instinct to endeavour to relieve the conception of Hell in any way that is open to us; but we shall be wise to attempt that only within the limits imposed by the truth of revelation, and as that has been understood and its meaning developed under the continued guidance manifested in the consensus of the Church's theology and its authoritative decisions; for however natural the desire to find such relief may be, to encourage human souls with a delusive hope would be the worst of crimes. On the other hand, it is a duty to set ourselves against the tendency, which seems natural to some persons, and from which Christian theologians and preachers have not always been free, to dogmatize beyond the limits of revelation, and to draw upon their imagination to describe and exaggerate the sufferings of Hell.

We have every right, therefore, to inquire what there is in Christian theology that allows for any mitigation of popular or exaggerated conceptions of Hell. The intense suffering of Hell seems to be sufficiently indicated by the frequent Scriptural references to the action of fire. It would seem, however, that the fires of Hell cannot possibly be of a material character, but can only represent the flames of conscience, the fires of remorse, or those evil desires which can only burn and never be relieved by satisfaction. Although the question has never been dogmatically decided, the tendency of Catholic theology has certainly been to maintain that the fires of Hell are material. This seems to many an unfortunate tendency, if not a childish mistake; for how, it may be asked, can physical fire have any effect on disembodied souls, or its action upon the body, with which the soul will eventually be clothed, be like the natural action of fire, since it is admitted it will not consume that body? It seems quite useless, therefore, to retain the idea of a material fire. We can well believe, however, that there is something behind this prevailing Catholic tendency which is worth further consideration. In the first place, although disembodied souls cannot be affected by fire as bodies can, and although the fire is obviously of such a nature that it does not destroy the body, its materiality may serve the purpose of restraining the soul through fear from venturing upon something which would certainly destroy it. Therefore the fire of Hell can be conceived as intended to keep souls from contact with God; fire is how the glory of God appears to souls that hate Him; so that we can at least say this about the fires of Hell, that dreadful as is the image they are meant to convey to the mind of what Hell can be, lost souls suffer far less than if they were allowed to draw near to God. The fires of Hell, then, prevent the destruction of the lost; and it is believed that whatever misery and unhappiness the souls of the lost may suffer, if they were given the choice they would always prefer their existence to non-existence. It has sometimes been made a charge of heartless cruelty against some Christian theologians that they have dared to declare that the sight of the damned in Hell would add to the bliss of the saved in Heaven. At first sight it does seem utterly contrary to everything that we expect in a spiritually advanced or intensely sympathetic soul to learn that it could derive any satisfaction from the sufferings of others, however wicked. It should be remembered, however, that this idea is

HELL

derived from the Scripture itself, where it is declared that those who receive the mark of the beast are "tormented for ever in the presence of the holy angels, and in the presence of the Lamb." And yet, what at first sight seems so dreadful, contains within it surely a certain assurance: if the contemplation of the souls in Hell wakes no pity in the sight of Heaven, if indeed Hell is able to exist when God is Love, and He is able to contemplate, as He must, the condition of the lost, this enables us to believe that there is nothing in the sufferings of Hell which need cause pity or should waken sympathy. It is difficult to know just how we can reconcile this complacency with the deprivation of the vision of God or the sufferings of souls shut up to the outer darkness and within the eternal fire; and it is hardly enough to appeal to the justice of their punishment, or to the fact that it is their own choice; but if the love of God can allow this, and the souls in bliss can contemplate it, we may be perfectly certain that there is no need to pity the souls in Hell, whatever their sufferings may be.

Perhaps some further light is thrown upon this difficulty if we remember that it is not only the penalty of pain, but the penalty of deprivation which constitutes the condition of Hell. It would be well to remind ourselves that the word "damnation" only means loss, although that loss is nothing less dreadful than the loss of the vision of God. For the idea that the souls in Hell are deprived of God brings a certain relief; for although to the estimate of the redeemed and the blessed this would be a most intolerable punishment, it is precisely this the souls in Hell deliberately desire; namely, to shut God out of their thoughts, to get rid of His presence, His inspiration, His illumination,

HELL

and to make themselves impervious to His appeal. To be in Hell must entail being entirely without God. Now that condition must bring with it an eternal deadening of soul and therefore some deprivation of personality; for if God were utterly to withdraw Himself from the human soul it would have the effect of working something approximating to a constitutional change in its consciousness and personality. We cannot deny to the souls that are in Hell consciousness or will, for they are there by their own will, and it is their consciousness that makes it Hell; but we need not import into the idea of Hell that awful pain which would smite upon the mind eager to see the face of God if it were told that this could never be granted. There is nothing in Hell corresponding to that awful pain of conscience which a soul knows when it recognizes that it has sinned not only against light, but against love, not only against itself, but against the Holy Spirit; for there is no penitence in Hell. Therefore, there are pains which are conceivably worse than those of Hell, and we have the sanction to believe that not all pains there are of the same intensity for all; there are degrees in the punishment of Hell. It must therefore be possible to regard the souls in Hell with no more concern than one looks upon coals burning in a fire; it is their will to be there, they have not a moment's wish to be anywhere else, they have no pains of conscience, no grief for being deprived of God. Their condition may perhaps be conceived as morally analogous to that of the incurably insane; sad as their condition is, it cannot be to them what it appears to those who possess their reason. Body, soul and spirit, the lost must eternally remain, but something has been subtracted from them, which must make them very different from even the worst human beings this world has known. We cannot say Hell is not a misery to such, but they have fallen in love with misery; not only have they said: "Evil, be thou my good," and "Darkness, be thou my light," but "Wretchedness, be thou my joy"; whatever their sufferings be, they prefer them to any other alternative. We can remember also that if eternal life, although it is everlasting, is not to be conceived as the multiplication of time, it must mean an experience for the soul quite different from anything conveyed to our minds in their present state by the idea of that which lasts for ever: if Heaven is to be measured by intensity of experience rather than by extension of time, we must think of Hell in the same way. There is no need to increase the sufferings of Hell by making one of its conditions the tedium of unending time; from which the bliss of Heaven is entirely free. There is no more time in Hell than in Heaven; both are in eternity. So while we have to consider that their condition is as fixed and as unalterable as all else in eternity, there is no need to burden the idea of Hell with anything contained in the notion of extended time.

But far more important, and much safer, than these mitigating suggestions, is the consideration of the question for whom Hell is prepared, and who are likely to find themselves there. In our Lord's own words the wicked are bidden to depart into the everlasting fire prepared for the devil and his angels. This declaration carries with it the relief that Hell was never prepared for human souls at all, and also seems to indicate that no one will ever go to Hell save for some sin equal to that of the fallen angels. There is, therefore, no warrant for the idea that the vast majority of mankind are bound to go to Hell. Such a notion has been erroneously inferred, either through heretical doctrines of predestination, whereby the mass of mankind have been conceived as decreed for Hell even before they were created; or because it was deemed necessary in order to reach Heaven to have attained on earth an explicit faith in God, the Incarnation, and the atoning Death of Christ. This demand would consign to Hell all the heathen, both before and since Christ came into the world. But that the heathen can be saved, without ever having heard of Christ at all, is fortunately a doctrine tenaciously held by the Catholic Church. We shall have to find place for a further discussion of what is meant by implicit faith, but there is a grace which can produce contrition and charity, of which even the heathen are capable, and this same grace makes it possible for them to share in the beatific vision, even though they have never heard the name of Christ, and even though their ideas of God are imperfect or erroneous. Indeed, it needs to be clearly affirmed, no soul will ever go to Hell merely through ignorance or error; we can go further and say, no soul will go to Hell merely through original sin, or indeed merely through sin at all, whatever its gravity. It must be said emphatically, and can be said with the full authority of the Catholic Church, no soul will ever be lost but for impenitence, conscious rebellion against God and the determined refusal of His grace. Therefore, for any soul to go to Hell demands that it must have had grace offered to it and known that it is grace; it must have heard the voice of God and known that it is the voice of God; it must have had Christ's salvation offered to it, and have known something of what that meant for Christ to offer and the soul to receive, and then, in full view of all that the choice entails, have rejected it and turned away. That, and nothing else, will ever send a soul to Hell, for it is that which creates inevitable Hell for the soul. Indeed, it needs to be said that it is not the heathen, or even those pagan souls which now unfortunately can be found within Christendom, for whom we need to be concerned, but rather for those who have seen the light of Christ, have received the grace of God, and who know the conditions of the world to come; for if they turn away, how is it possible to renew them unto repentance, and if they neglect so great salvation, how shall they escape? It is for those who have known the Christian revelation that Hell becomes more of a dreadful possibility; if they reject that, then their sin is like that of Lucifer and they receive a similar destiny. There is therefore no reason whatever to believe that the vast majority of mankind are destined for Hell.

It has, however, to be remembered that, according to Catholic doctrine, there are some souls who have never themselves sinned, yet who must fail to attain Heaven, because they have never received regenerating grace through Baptism, namely unbaptized infants. Although they are said to be in Hell because they are deprived of the vision of God and cannot, therefore, be in Heaven, strictly they are in Limbo, where, it is held, they do not suffer any pain, but, up to the limit of their own natural powers, are perfectly happy, and may, therefore, be considered as somewhat in the condition of merely animal souls which, as we can perceive, often enjoy a very happy existence. In the same condition, it is believed, are all those unbaptized adults who have failed to develop rational or moral powers. For, it must be remembered, that according to the Scholastic Theology, there is no rational development in the life to come. An

HELL

endeavour has been made by some, even Catholic thinkers, to extend this Limbo of the unbaptized to include all those who, though they have developed a full rational life, have never known saving grace, but have been faithful to what light they possessed, and lived according to what law they knew. This would doubtless relieve many of the heathen and vast numbers who have lived in Christendom without Christ, from the danger of going to Hell, and, at first sight, it seems unfortunate that the Catholic Church should have condemned this opinion. But the rejection of this idea has not been undertaken in order to shut up all such souls to the certainty of Hell, but rather to open to them the possibility of Heaven; for it is believed they are capable of an implicit faith which is sufficient to prepare them for the vision of God.

Further, although there has been an unfortunate readiness among some Christians to consign all those who have never heard the Gospel, and many who seem to have refused it, to certain Hell, we cannot, as a matter of theological certainty, assume the damnation of a single soul; for although some Catholic thinkers have held that our Lord's words concerning "the son of perdition" compel us to believe that this was the fate of Judas, others maintain that even such a description does not contain a decree of final damnation. We ought, therefore, never to assume that any living soul is bound for Hell; it is not even possible dogmatically to affirm that there is at present a single soul in Hell; all that the Catholic faith demands is that Hell is certain for those who die impenitent, while not even the most saintly soul, apart from some special divine revelation, can be certain of Heaven.

Heaven and Hell both remain, therefore, possibilities, not actualities; and possibilities for all

HELL

souls capable of reason or grace. Thus the Catholic doctrine of Hell remains a warning rather than an informing doctrine. At the same time the possibility of some souls, and in particular of my soul, going to Hell, is dreadfully open. And there may be those who will maintain that if Hell were even only barely possible, and for one solitary soul, then God never ought to have created man with a freedom that might have led to such consequences. The sufficient answer to that objection is surely this: God cannot be inhibited from proposing His blessed purpose for myriads of human souls, because in the exercise of that freedom without which Heaven could not be chosen, some might choose Hell; for such a condition would deprive God Himself of freedom. Indeed, the answer can go to the other extreme, for it can be affirmed that if all souls were lost save one, and only that soul was brought to eternal glory, the purpose thus achieved for one would more than outweigh the purpose refused by all the rest, so entirely does Heaven by its glory outbalance Hell.

IX

WHAT DETERMINES DESTINY?

IF man's eternal destiny holds such divergent possibilities as Heaven and Hell, it becomes of enormous importance to discover what it is that determines the character of that destiny. The answers that theology has made seem to be clear and have often been confidently made; but, on examination, they not only reveal many difficulties, but leave the issues still somewhat obscure.

The sole determinant of destiny has sometimes been ascribed simply to the divine decree; on the other hand, it has been made to depend entirely upon the free choice of the individual soul. Catholic Theology condemns and reprobates Calvinism; for that system makes everything determined only by the divine choice, and logically has to assume that some souls were predestined to Hell before they were born. But Catholic Theology has been able to do little more than maintain that predestination leaves human freedom unimpaired, without showing how these two operations can be reconciled. The Scriptures clearly and constantly refer the destiny of souls to the divine determination, but they as obviously assume that man is free to choose and is entirely responsible if he fails to avail himself of the divine provision of salvation, which is conceived to be sufficient for all, and is declared to be divinely willed for all.

It might be thought that the problem could be solved by the discovery that the concern of Scripture is not so much with who are elected as what they are elected to; since that is often stated to

WHAT DETERMINES DESTINY?

be to entire sanctification or to special service, rather than to bare salvation. Yet if this distinction can be pressed, the question still remains what it is that determines scarcely being saved from being almost saved (which latter really means being altogether lost), and therefore constitutes the awful difference between Heaven and Hell.

It might perhaps be wondered what objection there is, apart from Scriptural statements whose bearing is either obscure or unfathomable, to making the divine provision sufficient for the salvation of all, and then leaving everything else to human choice, as Arminianism, the historic alternative to Calvinism, was content to do. Catholicism indeed distinctly affirms that sufficient grace is given to enable every soul to attain salvation, but, where that salvation is actually attained, it assumes the action of efficacious grace. The issue narrows down, but still remains: What is it that determines the passage from sufficient to efficacious grace? If the link between the two is human choice, then salvation seems to depend ultimately upon human will rather than upon divine grace; if efficacious grace is bestowed as a reward for making full use of sufficient grace, then everything seems, in the last analysis, to depend upon human merit. Catholicism certainly demands a place for human merit; it regards salvation as both bestowed by God and won by man; but Protestantism in general, and Calvinism in particular, repudiate salvation by works, ascribe everything to grace, and therein thus seem to be nearer to the emphasis of Scripture, which certainly traces salvation to the grace of God and makes it impossible of attainment apart from grace.

It looks as if, at this point, an easy solution is within grasp, for surely salvation has two essentials,

WHAT DETERMINES DESTINY?

not one: grace and merit, the divine gift and human co-operation with the divine gift; neither is effectual without the other. Has not the difficulty therefore been created by referring to either element as a determinant when both are equally necessary? This may be so, but it is more than curiosity that desires to know precisely in what proportion, and particularly in what order these two elements unite. We want to know in order to instruct men what they ought to do, as well as to know what we ourselves must do to make our calling and election sure. Something must take place if the transition from sufficient to efficacious grace is to be made; what is it, and who does it? If that which makes the difference between sufficiency and efficiency, between what *can* and what *does* effect salvation, is also a grace, as the term efficacious grace seems to imply, then that again must be simply God's gift, and there seems no room left for human action; and then, why God does not give to all souls what they need for the actual attainment of salvation remains a dark and perplexing question.

If we turn to find a solution in the operation of faith, we may hope to find the problem further narrowed down. In order that grace may be efficacious, the purpose of grace, namely, the bringing of the soul to eternal glory, must be revealed, faith must be used to accept this revelation, and it is this faith that justifies. Here, then, we seem to discern the critical determinant of destiny. Is this faith man's meritorious act? The Scripture seems to state, and Catholic Theology teaches, that even this faith is not of ourselves; it is the gift of God. This seems to throw the determinant issue again solely on to the side of God, so that it seems as if it depended only on His choice who shall receive

WHAT DETERMINES DESTINY?

this essential gift. And if we turn to external observation, then the gift of faith seems obviously to rest solely upon divine selection. For, first of all, faith must depend upon God revealing to man His purpose of eternal glory and the means of attaining it; which, in turn, seems to depend upon Christ's coming into the world, the obtaining of our redemption by the sacrifice of Calvary, and both being made known to all mankind. If we can include the revelation made known to the Jews as disclosing something of the nature of God, promising a fuller salvation through the Messiah, and providing in their sacrifices an anticipation of His sacrificial death, there is still the question as to how many of the Jews can be said to have died in faith, having seen the promises afar off; while outside the chosen race there remains to be considered the vast mass of heathendom sunk in the darkness of ignorance, error and superstition. But even since Christ's coming, the knowledge of God's nature, His purpose of salvation, and the means of attaining that through faith in Christ, have been dependent upon the Church's evangelistic efforts, which have failed even yet to reach anything like the majority of mankind. Further, that knowledge has often been inadequately presented or imperfectly understood. Within the most illuminated areas of Christendom many can be met with who have most distorted views of Christianity, and who, because of these, have rejected not only the Church and Christ, but any revelation, and even the goodness or the very existence of God. Moreover, when we come to know intimately many persons, believers and unbelievers, why the one actually believes and the other does not is often shrouded in complete obscurity. If the man who believes is asked why he does so, he will probably

WHAT DETERMINES DESTINY?

declare that it is impossible for him to do anything else; and if the unbeliever be asked why he does not believe, he will generally affirm that for him belief is impossible. If the difference between them is explained as due to the fact that one man has the gift of faith while it has been withheld from the other, the question then becomes acute how far this is due to divine choice and how far to human action. On the hypothesis that faith is necessary to salvation the vast majority of mankind seem shut out from all hope, and this solely by the decision of God to withhold from them what is essential.

Some of these difficulties might, perhaps, be removed if we knew precisely what is involved in faith, and what must precede its bestowal. Inquiry in this direction, however, soon reveals the fact that how much it is necessary to believe in order to be saved, and what are the psychological elements in faith, are questions that remain in considerable obscurity. Since the Reformation the meaning and efficacy of faith have remained points of controversy between Protestantism and Catholicism. In opposition to the insistence of the Mediæval Church upon various religious observances as necessary to salvation, the Reformation took the stand that justification was by faith alone. And by justification the Reformers meant being reckoned righteous solely on the ground of the perfect substitutionary work of Christ. Faith was therefore conceived as consisting in a simple and wholehearted trust in the efficacy of Christ's sacrifice; and this in theoretical isolation from the effect it might be expected to produce in the believer's character and conduct. This attitude seems to offend against two great statements of Scripture, namely: that faith without works is dead, and that faith without love

WHAT DETERMINES DESTINY?

profits nothing. It can be said without fear of contradiction that whatever may have been the belief of the early Reformers, the doctrine of a purely forensic justification, secured by faith alone, is no longer discoverable among Protestants, save perhaps in the case of a few obscure and ever-dwindling sects. The fact is that Protestant thought tends more and more to swing to the other extreme, and to hold that character and good works are the only means of justification; as the common phrase has it, it is not what a man believes, but what he does that matters; if popular religion is not in process of going farther and maintaining that it is not even what a man is, but what he does, that matters; it is not a man's personal character, but his social conduct which determines his salvation.

The Catholic resistance to the Reformation position has been to maintain, first, that faith has an intellectual content, and, secondly, that it brings sanctifying grace. This, however, does not leave the issue with which we are at present concerned so clear as might be desired. In the first place, the faith that brings sanctifying grace cannot be a mere intellectual assent, whether that assent be that of the natural reason accepting the fact of God's existence, or the submission to the authority of the Church with the acceptance of all the doctrines that it proclaims to be necessary to salvation. The fact that faith is stated to be the gift of God, and that it must go on to work the transformation of the soul in charity towards God and man, shows that it is something quite other than mere reason or mere belief on authority. There must be something at work which transforms the soul and makes it fit for the presence of God, and this is commonly said to be grace. Now grace has been analysed into " sufficient " and " efficacious " grace, and it

WHAT DETERMINES DESTINY?

has been denied that it leaves no place for human choice and merit, or that the action of grace is irresistible and destroys human freedom or the need for co-operation. But how these two interact, and which is at any moment determinant for any soul, it still seems impossible to decide. Suppose we try to present the whole movement by which a man comes to attain salvation. Following the guidance of his reason, which is, of course, itself a gift of God, a man comes to believe that God exists and will reveal Himself to those who seek Him. If that man then diligently seeks God, He will reveal Himself and the means of grace necessary to salvation. If the man accepts these, and is faithful to all the conditions, this will bring him at last to Heaven. But at every stage there is the question of fidelity to what has been revealed, and on that everything still hangs. Saving faith, therefore, seems to embrace at least four things: intellectual assent, trust, a supernatural gift, and fidelity; they are *all* necessary; but how these work together to secure final salvation cannot be stated in general terms in such a way as to show where the actual determinant lies at any particular moment for any individual soul, and no individual soul can know it even in his own case. Human freedom and divine provision intertwine so closely and continuously that we cannot tell where one begins and the other ends. It can only be stated dogmatically, on the one hand, that no one will be lost save through his own fault; and, on the other, that no one will be saved without divine grace. The impossibility of finding a complete intellectual solution to the problem is probably due to the divine economy in withholding a complete revelation, which better serves the divine purpose; for it urges everyone to work out his own salvation with fear and trembling, to leave nothing

WHAT DETERMINES DESTINY?

to chance, to take no risks, and to use every available means of grace: the gift of reason, the gift of faith, the gift of the sacraments and the gift of prayer. Whether one is in the faith, whether one is in a state of grace, whether one's salvation is assured, no one can actually know unless by some supernatural revelation. We are left in a position which bids us do everything we know to be a duty, as if our salvation depended upon that alone; and yet, when we have done all, to know that we must trust simply to the mercy of God. Thus far, and no farther, can theology take us; and that it can do no more than bid us make our calling and election sure, and to work out the salvation which God works in us, must remain its last word; and the recognition that no revelation has been given of the determining factor, or sufficient to provide a reconciliation of divine predestination and human freedom, can only be referred to the inscrutable judgment of divine wisdom.

There are, however, one or two problems which can be cleared up within the area marked out by divine revelation. The first problem concerns those who are living within the full light of Christianity. Here the duty of rational inquiry into the proofs for the existence of God, the examination of the claims of Christ, and the submission to the authority of the Church, become more urgent, and involve everyone in serious responsibility; while to neglect the means of grace in prayer and sacrament, to refuse to obey the Church or a divine vocation, to excuse oneself from responding fully to the claims of God or man, would certainly imperil one's salvation. Therefore it almost looks as if the area of the Christian revelation, its personal acceptance, the provision of the privileges of membership in the Church, only increased, respectively, and in

WHAT DETERMINES DESTINY?

increasing proportion, the peril of losing salvation. For if a soul is at any point unfaithful, it would seem to be in danger of being lost; and no one can safely assure himself at any moment that there is no real danger for him. But there is a counter-consideration. The more grace is yielded to, step by step, the more it secures for the soul the further aid of grace, until at last a point is reached where no possibility of falling away remains. We can only know that this point has been reached when we see God face to face in the beatific vision, for that will unite us for ever to Him. Some souls, no doubt, reach that point of indefectible salvation before they depart from this life; which would, of course, be outwardly signified if they received the beatific vision here on earth; but whether any souls have attained this vision while in the flesh, or whether any soul has been assured of the grace of final perseverance, is ordinarily beyond decision, and belongs to the realm of the supernatural.

Something, moreover, needs to be said to lighten the problem which arises owing to the present confused condition of Christendom. There are undoubtedly many souls to-day who are misled by the false principles which dominate most of our modern thought, or repelled by inadequate or poorly presented teaching concerning articles of the Catholic faith, and who have therefore rejected important doctrines necessary to salvation. Others, confused by the divided state of the Church, have found refuge in heretical sects. Others refuse to acknowledge the authority of the one Church; or they are unable to concede this authority to the Roman communion only, feeling its claim to unity to be negatived by the failure to exhibit other essential marks of the Church. Others, again, are in doubt concerning their vocation, or their fulfil-

WHAT DETERMINES DESTINY?

ment of their duties and obligations, and almost in despair concerning their character. What can be said about all these? To demand a standard of absolute fidelity as necessary to salvation would, for the most sensitive souls, destroy all hope. It could be answered that fidelity is only expected up to the light one actually possesses, that grace is refused to no one save to those who, at some stage or other, positively refuse grace. But since no one who knows himself could be assured that he had always attained absolute fidelity, it needs also to be said that it is not mere failure that imperils salvation, but only rebellion against truth and deliberate refusal of the grace of God.

Similar principles have to be applied if we now widen our concern beyond those souls who are living under the light of faith and have access to the means of grace, and consider the condition of those who are unaware of the authority of the Church or the grace revealed in Christ, and have even only the dimmest knowledge of God. What hopes of Heaven can we have for them, if faith is necessary, since for them faith seems impossible? Nevertheless, the Catholic Church teaches that we may have hope for souls outside Christendom, even when sunk in the depths of paganism or heathendom. It is believed that there is open to them the possibility of attaining an implicit faith. It is held to be possible for a man to make acts of faith, contrition and charity, which shall open Heaven to him at the last, even though he may know nothing of revealed religion, of the laws of God, or of the Christian salvation. He will be judged according to the light he has seen and the law that he knows. And yet even in his case what procures his salvation is not merely his own effort, but divine grace, and that the grace which is resident in Christ, and whose

WHAT DETERMINES DESTINY?

nature and extent is made manifest through the Cross. Indeed, we may define implicit faith at its lowest as a man's sense of something higher than himself and his desire to be like that, so long as that desire moves him to make every effort possible to come in contact with what is higher than himself and to attain it. This implicit faith is, nevertheless, of such a character that if the man who possesses it were to know the historic revelation of God, be presented with the claims of Christ and His Church, or receive a divine call, he would obey it. It is of the same virtual content as a full explicit faith and only needs the revelation of the content of faith, to bring it out. But even then it is assumed that some exercise this implicit faith and some do not. What is it that makes the difference? Is implicit faith as much the gift of God as explicit faith? Then if so, does God withhold the gift from some? We are back at the same old question. If we say that it is fidelity to that reason, intuition or ideals which all men possess, that brings the reward of faith, it then places a burden of responsibility upon man's side that no man could feel certain he had ever fully discharged. If we could make the reward of implicit faith depend merely upon sincerity, and interpret that to include a man's willingness to face all the facts of life, to pursue all the implications of his own thought, to acknowledge his defects, his needs and his desires, although this seems to be the lowest possible necessity as a prelude to faith, how many who know themselves would feel that they could plead that, whatever the nature of the explicit faith they had attained, they at least had always been, therefore, sincere, and could face the Judgment confident on that issue?

Christian theology can, however, take us a little

farther. It assures us that God presses His salvation upon every man, and that no man will fail of ultimate salvation unless at some point or other he positively refuses grace. That man can at any point refuse grace is implied in the Catholic rejection of the idea that grace is not irresistible. This same principle governs the conditions where, through knowledge of the Christian faith and in contact with the Church, there is the possibility of attaining to explicit faith. If this offers greater opportunities of light and grace in this life, with the possibility of attaining a higher place in glory in the life to come, it brings with it a greater responsibility and a heavier condemnation if the grace that is offered is not responded to. It is because greater knowledge brings greater responsibility that our Lord so often warns people in the Gospels that it is not the mere knowledge of Himself, not the acceptance of theological truth, not high expression of personal devotion, not even having done great work for Him, that are sufficient of themselves to gain an entrance into the Kingdom, but only the doing of the Father's will. This all-determining condition must depend upon how far the will of God is known, but it shows that whatever a man's opportunities are, the same principle is at work. No one will therefore miss Heaven through ignorance or through mere failure, but only through deliberate rebellion against the light actually received. The coming of light to the soul at any stage does not mean that it deprives a man of perfect freedom to decide whether or not he will follow the light. But if more light is seen, and more grace is sought in order to live up to it, then still more light will be given, but always with more responsibility.

Some Catholic theologians appeal to God's foreknowledge to explain why, within the area of

WHAT DETERMINES DESTINY?

Christian light, God seems to bestow more grace on some souls than on others. It must be because He knows just how any soul will respond to grace, and He therefore withholds higher grace from some only because He knows they would refuse it, and would thus fall under heavier condemnation. Therefore He gives only such light as souls will actually follow. This suggestion promises some further relief to our problem, for it explains why some souls do not seem to have seen further light or to have been given higher grace: their salvation is secure, though they will only attain a lower stage of glory than others whose faithfulness was foreknown.

This solution has not, however, commended itself to all Catholic theologians; and naturally, for if God's foreknowledge were held to determine every offer of grace, it would seem to involve that no one who had attained to the possibility of salvation could ever so refuse grace that he would be entirely lost; for, in such a case, the grace that would have been refused would have been withheld; whereas it has always been held by Catholic thought that even when a soul is in a state of grace which would secure salvation if at that moment the soul died, if that soul lived it might still fall from grace. On this theory, the only souls that would ever be lost would be those who were presented with the grace that made salvation barely possible, and who then refused it. Once past that stage, however, salvation would be assured, and all that would be left open to determination would be the differing degrees of glory that could be attained.

Yet if, on the other hand, we were to suppose that, within the area of light sufficient for salvation, with the coming of fresh light or the call to a higher stage of obedience, the offer of a greater grace might be refused, and this refusal lead to the complete loss of salvation, then souls outside this area would seem to be in a safer position, and implicit faith and invincible ignorance would seem the only sure way to salvation. The proclamation of Christianity, the presence of the Catholic Church, the claims of the religious life, would only seem to place souls in a greater possibility of peril, and a short life would seem much less dangerous than a long one. It could be maintained in reply, that while there is no stage attainable in this life at which a soul could not be lost, and the higher the point from which a soul fell the greater the fall, yet the higher a soul can rise, the less likelihood there is of falling.

If none of these suggestions enables us to discover what it is that determines salvation, or to resolve the antinomy between predestination and free will, it might seem a solution to hold, as some New Testament statements seem to allow, that predestination imples nothing more than God's personal will to salvation, and the laying down of the conditions on which it is attainable, or that election is only to special service or peculiar sanctity. But even if this left the attainment of salvation to be determined purely by the human choice to accept grace, who would actually be saved would still be known to God beforehand by virtue of His omniscience. Yet to make predestination depend solely upon foreknowledge would seem to empty it of reality; while if predestination does not depend upon foreknowledge, but is a free choice of God as to who shall be saved, it seems to leave no freedom to man. If the predestination of some souls to grace leaves it still open to them to refuse grace, it can hardly be called predestination. Nevertheless, Catholic theology contents itself with maintaining that there is such a thing as predestination, and yet

WHAT DETERMINES DESTINY?

that souls can refuse grace; and, indeed, that if any soul is lost it will be lost solely for refusing grace and rebelling against the known will of God. Indeed, one great school of Catholic Theology maintains that, while predestination does mean the predetermination of all men's acts, nevertheless man is free in those acts; grace is not irresistible, and if any man is lost it is his own fault.

It may well be that the solution of this problem lies beyond human wisdom because the material for its solution has not been revealed. It may be that no real revelation is possible to us in our present state because it could not be made in general principles that would be capable of application by us to individual souls; a full solution would involve revealing the intricate action of divine grace and human choice as it took place in every individual soul. It may be, however, that the crux of the problem is to be found in the fact that we are bound to consider the divine foreknowledge from the standpoint of time, whereas the knowledge of God must be beyond time altogether; so that it is strictly incorrect to say that God knows a thing before it happens, since with Him there is no before or after. For God, therefore, what we call predestination does not really precede man's act. In the ultimate analysis predestination would turn out to be nothing but the divine judgment upon man's act, simultaneously delivered and expressed in man's act. It would mean that all human actions incur and register the divine judgment, the human and the divine elements being both absolutely free, but absolutely coincident.

No farther can the human mind penetrate; but with the assurance that God's will and man's freedom are neither frustrated, and that no soul will be lost save by wilful action and final rebellion,

WHAT DETERMINES DESTINY?

we must content ourselves with the practical conclusions that are sufficient for the direction of all our lives. Heaven is possible for all, and therefore Christian theology holds the widest hopes for all; but it is the Church's duty to make known to all not only the good news of salvation, but the highest glory that God's grace makes possible to any soul. Nevertheless, any soul may be lost at any point in life; so that if it is asked what we must do to be saved, the answer, although simple to state: " Believe on the Lord Jesus Christ and thou shalt be saved; " while allowing for an implicit as well as an explicit faith, that omission involves that a soul must do everything it can: be faithful to all it knows, avail itself of every means of grace, obey every command, keep constant watch against temptation, and strive for greater charity to God and man.

There is no safety in calculating upon any minimum necessary to salvation; such an attitude would itself betray an utter lack of grace. The utmost we can do is the least we can afford; the highest attainment is the best security. But when we have done all, we have no assurance of salvation, save through the merits of Christ and the grace of God. We must all depend at last upon that which never for a moment must we dare presume upon: the mercy of God.

X

OUR RELATIONSHIP WITH THE DEPARTED

THE state and condition of the souls who have departed this life, and the possibility of reestablishing relationships with them, has become a question in which our generation is vitally interested; and this interest has been aroused and quickened for many by the discoveries of psychical research, and by the belief which spiritualistic practices are said to confirm, that we can actually get into communication with those who have died, in such a way as not only to gain a scientific assurance of the survival of personality, but detailed information concerning the spiritual world. We have previously examined the claims of mediumistic spiritualism, and have found reason to conclude that the claim to be brought into touch with departed souls through such means is not supported by adequate proof of their identity; that it is open to deception through the possibility of impersonation by other spirits, and those perhaps of a demoniacal order; it builds the hope of immortality on a false foundation and may be deliberately used to convey wrong notions of the other life; and its practice so often has a deteriorating effect upon mentality and morality, that it is dangerous and is best left alone, save for purely scientific inquiry by scientific persons.

A more intimate relationship, and one that at first may seem less open to objection and danger, is the communication that it is claimed can be received from departed souls by means of automatic writing. In this case we have the promise of a more direct contact, since no living medium has to be used, neither is a medium in the spirit world generally necessary; and mostly, therefore, automatic writing is only practised in order to get in touch with some beloved soul recently departed. Nevertheless, on examination, it is found to have similar, or even greater, dangers for the inquirer. The practice of surrendering one's conscious control, whether it means surrendering it only to the subconscious mind, or to another personality, is a very questionable practice, and bound to be fraught with danger to the mental constitution. It is still possible, that even if a spirit does then control one's mind and write through one's hand, it may not be the spirit of the departed person; for the proofs of identity forthcoming through automatic script generally appear inadequate, at least to a third person; and even when they amount to an imitation of the handwriting, or the use of favourite expressions employed by the spirit when alive, these are either referable to sub-conscious activity on the part of the automatic writer, or if to a communicating spirit, then the absence of other knowledge which might be expected, the evasion of test questions, and the general disposition displayed are often highly suspicious. For, in this method also, there is no safeguard against an impersonating spirit, and therefore one of a possibly immoral character and with an evil purpose. The surrender of the mind to another, even when it is only to some spirit with whom on earth there was the closest union, would go beyond anything that true union between human spirits ever approaches, or could demand, and would be in itself a danger to the personality; while if it opens up the possibility of possession by an evil spirit, however remote that may be, and however much the fact of demon-possession may be doubted, the danger is too serious to be trifled with. But if we were to allow that any residuum of the information which has accumulated through mediums or through automatic writing concerning the life of the departed was authentic, we should still be faced with the fact that the information thus available lacks consistency, contains frequent contradictions, is suspiciously vague, or hopelessly trivial. Taking the evidence as a whole, it must at least be said that the veil still remains unlifted. Even if connection has been established, it has provided us with nothing that can be dignified with the description of a new revelation.

Nevertheless, we cannot rest content with this merely negative position : humanity evidently craves something more. It is sometimes declared that spiritualism would never have had such a vogue if the doctrine of the Communion of Saints had not been so neglected by Protestantism ; and it is therefore implied that the Catholic belief concerning the other life not only provides an adequate bulwark against the seductions of spiritualism, but satisfies all legitimate cravings for the continuance of spiritual relationship with souls now in the other world. It is to be feared that the Catholic prohibition of spiritualism is effective because of obedience to the Church's ruling, rather than that the popular understanding of the relationship with departed souls which Catholic practice establishes satisfies the natural craving of the bereaved heart when death has suddenly put an end to close attachment and intimate intercourse between two souls here on earth. It cannot be expected that death should make no difference : death itself, and not merely the sense of bereavement,

OUR RELATIONSHIP WITH THE DEPARTED

must be abolished before the salvation of humanity is consummated. If the communion of saints could establish such a relationship that nothing more could be desired, we should have nothing left to hope for. At the same time it must be admitted that Catholic theology, which gives us a mere outline of principles, and Catholic practice (being concerned mainly with the spiritual benefit of the departed), can be presented or understood in a way that seems to do little to compensate for what the bereaved soul misses so sorely, namely, intimate human contact and intelligible intercourse. But, since there is misunderstanding, it needs to be set forth what precisely the Catholic conception allows us to believe concerning the possibility of establishing any kind of contact with souls now dwelling in the other world? In the first place, it allows us to believe that we can get into touch with the saints; but apart from their occasional and miraculous appearance to certain persons, and the special concern which the adoption of a patron saint may be believed to secure, neither of which can be guaranteed to be free from some degree of subjective imagination, the only contact generally open and completely to be trusted is that of invoking their prayers. No doubt it would be very interesting, as well as informing, if anyone of us could get into such personal contact, say, with the Apostle Paul or St. Francis, that we could clear up difficulties concerning their opinion and wishes while on earth, or learn what they think and desire in the fuller light in which they now stand. If we could establish actual communication with any lesser saint, we should surely be able to gain much needed information concerning the conditions of the heavenly life, or, what it is sometimes so anxiously desired to know, the happiness or destiny of someone who has recently departed. But as a general rule, there has been no claim, or the Church does not guarantee any certainty, that revelation of this character has ever been given or is really obtainable. Sometimes the cult of a particular saint will become popular for a certain time, in certain quarters, or for certain purposes, and thanksgiving may be offered to that saint in the belief that through his intercession our prayers have been actually heard, and thus a feeling of real contact and intimate relationship may be established. But these are pious opinions which, although they need not be discouraged, at the same time cannot be regarded as certain.

There is the further difficulty that it is necessary, at least to those who have not been brought up to the practice of invoking the saints, to justify even its general effectuality. How can we be sure, it may be asked, that the saints in heaven can hear us at all? Has the Church any right to specify or power to assure us that there are certain persons to whom requests for prayer can be properly addressed? Perhaps there is now less need than previously to consider any objection to the invocation of saints on the ground that prayer can be addressed only to God, and that to invoke the saints is idolatry. Prayer is a term that has wide meanings: we use it not only of a request addressed to God, but also, for instance, of a petition addressed to Parliament. Similarly, when praying to the saints is being discussed, it should be understood that that is a loose expression which more strictly means, asking the saints to pray for us. Now since it is a pious and unquestioned custom amongst all Christians to ask our friends, and especially those who are known to be given to prayer, to pray for us if we are in special difficulty or need, it would be difficult to maintain that they could no longer receive such requests or make intercession for us, because they had died, if we had reason to believe that they were now in the actual presence of God; unless we held the idea that heaven's inhabitants were far removed from human concern; which would be inadmissible, if heaven consists in being near to the heart and mind of God. But if we may take the general principle, which would allow us to ask the intercessions of the departed, as now widely admitted, the question might still be raised, why it should be only the saints who are invoked.

It must be understood at the outset that the Catholic Church nowhere claims that the canonization of a saint is of the nature of an infallible decision that that soul has reached the state of beatitude; still less does it claim that only the canonized saints have reached such a state. The theory behind canonization, for the purpose of invocation, can be shown, however, on general spiritual principles to be completely valid. We are not here considering the process of canonization, the evidence of sanctity that is demanded, or the general type of character which modern Roman Catholic authorities seem to favour; though it should be mentioned that the process is at least searching, it is only undertaken when spontaneous devotion and popular demand have already paved the way; and if the evidence for complete orthodoxy or the possession of miraculous power may seem to some persons unnecessary or suspicious, they will at least be glad to know that the manifestation of heroic virtue is always regarded as the chief evidence of sanctity. But we can perhaps look for a general comprehension of indisputably spiritual principles which dictate that only those

OUR RELATIONSHIP WITH THE DEPARTED

who have reached a certain degree of proximity to God can be effectual intercessors, while only those who have attained an advanced spiritual outlook can be safely concerned again with mundane affairs. Sometimes we ourselves express the hope that our departed friends or loved ones do not actually know what is passing on earth, particularly the sorrow or shame which may have come to those whom they had greatly loved. We have a natural feeling that it would inevitably cloud their happiness if such knowledge were theirs. On the other hand, we know that God sees all and is concerned for all, and yet this does not in any way destroy His bliss. Therefore it follows that if only any soul now closely shares the mind and outlook of God, that soul might be able to be informed of what is happening here on earth without its happiness being thereby destroyed; indeed, by its close union with the mind of God the completely sanctified soul must be able to know what is passing on earth, or at least be able to have it revealed without disturbing its bliss. All that the Church claims in canonizing certain saints, and thus indicating that their prayers may be invoked, is that their character and life on earth manifested such a degree of sanctification that it is allowable to conclude that they would be allowed to receive our requests, since their minds would not be distracted, nor their spirits disturbed, by being informed of our needs and desires, while, since they are now numbered among the spirits of just men made perfect, their intercessions must be supremely effective. It is not in the power, nor is it in the desire of the Church, to prohibit prayer being addressed to others, who anyone may feel privately convinced have attained that same blessed condition, but where there is no public knowledge

OUR RELATIONSHIP WITH THE DEPARTED

that enables the Church to make any such pronouncement; a universal cult is only proclaimed where there is available evidence that there was an earthly example worthy of being imitated, and therefore some assurance of a heavenly state being reached where invocations can be received and intercession made. Sometimes those who believe that their departed friends, or some near relation, were so saintly that they would be open to receive a request for prayers, yet who wish to keep within the limits of the Church's assurance, will adopt the pious precaution of asking for their prayers through the introduction of some canonized saint, especially, for instance, through the Blessed Virgin, who is assuredly the Queen of saints and greatest of intercessors. There can be no objection to such a practice, and it does help to keep alive a sense of spiritual fellowship with those who have been to us such a blessing and help while on earth, where otherwise our memory of them, and the sense of their being alive, may all too easily fade away. Moreover, we can believe that even when their prayers are not requested, the saints in heaven—and it must be remembered that all who are in heaven are saints—are always interceding for the world, and, we may believe, particularly for the causes or souls with which they had a special concern when dwelling here on earth.

If even on these spiritual principles, and with this wider permission, the craving which some may feel for a greater intimacy or a continued contact with their departed friends and relatives is not satisfied, it may seem to be open to further disappointment by the general belief concerning the souls still in Purgatory. It is held that souls in this condition are neither in a position to receive our requests nor to be able to pray for us; they are so entirely concerned with the relationship between God and their own souls, which has yet to be perfected by the purification both of the stains which sin has left and of the love which is not yet perfected, that it is not only impossible for the thought of anyone else to enter their minds, but in their present condition it would be a serious distraction and hindrance. We have already indicated some reasons that would make this regulation against praying to souls in Purgatory not only spiritually valid, but humanly considerate, and these ought to be weighed against desires which would intrude our affairs upon departed souls, or, still more selfishly, summon their spirits back again to earth, even if it were held that either of these things were possible. What often constitutes the tragedy of death and accentuates the pain of bereavement is a mere selfish concern for our own loss, unrelieved by any consideration of the gain that may be theirs whom we profess so to love. If we cannot rise above our own grief, we should surely hesitate to force it upon those who have won their release from earthly pain and sorrow.

If, however, we may not receive the help of the prayers of those who are in Purgatory, it is held that they may receive the help of ours; and if so, that is one of the most unselfish and spiritual works of mercy that we can render. The Council of Trent, which, by the reticence of its Decree on Purgatory, refused to sanction many of the superstitions, and even gave no guarantee to many of the pious beliefs and practices which had grown up in the Middle Ages, was content to insist that such a place exists, and that souls undergoing its painful processes may be helped by our prayers, especially through the offering of the Sacrifice of the Mass on their behalf. It is a little difficult, at first sight, to see

OUR RELATIONSHIP WITH THE DEPARTED

how such intercession can really be a help to souls in Purgatory, if they themselves do not know that such prayers are being offered on their behalf, or that the sacrifice of Christ is being specially applied to their succour. But on further thought it will be seen that there is no more objection to their receiving help from prayers when they do not know that they are being offered than there is in the case of the living. It is part of the general dispensation of God's providence, who has made His creatures so spiritually dependent upon one another, that the prayer of one soul for another can often be more effective even than its own prayers for itself. This law is one of many that makes prayer so valuable for the sanctifying of human fellowship and at the same time protects prayer against the corruption of selfishness. It must be for the same reason that in Masses for the dead, even when they are offered for a particular individual, we are directed to pray always in the plural: rest eternal grant unto *them*, O Lord: and let light perpetual shine upon *them*. We might, however, conceive that the souls in Purgatory, being already so far advanced that they are concerned with nothing but the perfecting of their love, could derive little benefit from our prayers, when our condition is so far beneath any such preoccupation. But this is why prayer for souls in Purgatory is directed particularly to take the form of the application of the One Sacrifice to their need. It is believed that there may be a certain darkness possessing the minds of those who are in Purgatory; this is not only consequent upon their first vision of Christ, but they are so completely obsessed with desire to see the face of God, and this involves such suffering, because of the hindrance to this their sins have imposed, that they are perhaps not

OUR RELATIONSHIP WITH THE DEPARTED

always clear about their condition because of the pain it involves. At any rate they need to have presented to their minds, with constant reiteration, that Sacrifice to which they must look, both for their purification from the effects of sin and their perfection in love. It is the application to them of that Sacrifice which is their one hope, and we may reverently believe our union with Christ in the Mass enables us to direct this to their benefit, and it is therefore the greatest service we can render them. The impact of a Requiem on a soul for which it is offered must be to increase its hope and to centre all its desire upon the Crucified, and thus to prepare the soul for, and bring it nearer to, that final vision of God in which it can then for ever live and in it find eternal bliss, because it is pure enough to endure His holiness and delight in the glory of God.

It must be admitted, however, that when all has been said that can be, in regard to our possible contact, either with the canonized saints or with the souls of our own beloved departed, who we may hope are numbered among the worshipping hosts of Heaven, we still have to depend upon general principles that permit of little further application to individual conditions, and have to content ourselves with spiritual methods that do not seem to promise much conscious or certain contact with the spirits of the departed. The communion of saints, however firmly believed in, or assiduously cultivated, is not a practice which furnishes us with much material capable of providing a further revelation, nor does it often convey a sense of actual contact with those whom we would fain still feel near. It is not therefore surprising that in the case of the recent loss of anyone closely connected or passionately loved, the Catholic

OUR RELATIONSHIP WITH THE DEPARTED

conception of the relations possible with the departed should seem somewhat remote, vague and cold. But we must first of all confront ourselves with the consideration that *no* invocation of the saints, and *no* intercession for departed souls, the attitude hitherto taken up by extreme Protestantism, would leave us only worse off, while the promises of spiritualism are too specious to be trusted, and its methods too dangerous to be tried; though Protestantism will speedily have to make up its mind to which of these two practices it is going to allow the Christian people under its tuition to turn; for one or the other it will have to be. But a further advance along safe lines is open and promising. It can soon be discovered that if only more spiritual views of the heavenly life are adopted, if only Catholic theology and practice are recognized as intended to provide us merely with the framework which our own spiritual understanding must fill out, and if only our intercourse with the departed is sought in order to increase our spirituality, and for their spiritual benefit, there is a realm of rich and satisfying experience which promises more than the satisfaction of curiosity, or intercourse that would merely continue earthly relationships. A purely domestic or individual concern in the other world cannot be placed alongside the educative value of the communion of saints; though there is no reason why the experience of bereavement should not provide an introduction to the communion of saints and invest the heavenly life with much more reality and intimacy; as is, indeed, very often the case. On the other hand, it can be noticed that the interest in, and enthusiasm for spiritualism is often of a strangely temporary character, even when it is believed that most indubitable communication has been established

OUR RELATIONSHIP WITH THE DEPARTED

and when most wonderful revelations are declared to have been received. Somehow it all begins to wear thin, and even to become somewhat wearisome; though it needs to be recorded that not a few people have begun to take a living interest in Christianity through the alleged revelations of spiritualism, and some have gradually worked their way past its influence and beyond its methods to find something far more satisfying in Catholic faith and practice.

But if progress in a greater realization of the communion of the saints, or closer contact with our departed loved ones is to be promised or can be expected, it must be remembered that it will be established through spiritual growth and be dependent upon spiritual appreciation. The sense of God's presence is never a physical thing, but is due to a purely spiritual function apprehending a purely spiritual Being; even though that apprehension may become more vivid than anything our senses could register, and even though we have to use sensuous language to describe what it is like Similarly there is a contact with departed souls which is assuring and satisfying, that nevertheless owes nothing to visions seen or voices heard; indeed, it is not immediate contact with an individual soul at all; and yet it is something more intimate and understanding than any earthly experience of that could ever be.

It must be remembered, moreover, that any dependence for our attraction to the heavenly life on definite personal communication with the departed has not really found the innermost secret of Heaven's attraction. The heart of Heaven's attraction is the Sacred Heart, our Lord's humanity, the glory of His face and the love of His embrace; and all other things, even communion with the saints, or the re-knitting up of sundered friendships

OUR RELATIONSHIP WITH THE DEPARTED

and the restoration of separated loves are secondary to that. But in being made secondary they are not thereby made lower, less affectionate and satisfying than they were on earth; but by being sought through Him, with Him, and in Him, they are immensely heightened. Therefore it can soon be proved that those who desire to continue the loving relationships that death has ruthlessly broken may do so, in the first place, by making a habit of regular prayer for the soul departed, even though they content themselves, as the Church encourages us to do, with the general prayer for " eternal rest and light perpetual." For that will soon be found to hold far more than the words always convey; for they are a prayer that the soul departed may behold that light of glory for which the soul is athirst, and experience that rest which must indicate that the soul is at once, for ever, and perfectly, satisfied. If, moreover, we suppress any cravings for the re-establishment of earthly relationships which have now been broken, and which, on the Christian view of the other life, can never be restored, and rather remember the principal needs or the present occupation of the departed soul, namely, the unclouded worship and uninterrupted love of God, it will be found that by lifting up the soul in adoration of God, or, at the Eucharist, uniting in worship with angels and archangels, and with all the company of heaven, we shall be partaking in the worship for which our beloved are being prepared, or in which they are already occupied, and in that closer contact with God we shall find ourselves in closest contact with them. There may come to us at such times a sweet, mystic assurance not only that they are near to us, but that they are perfectly satisfied, since they see Him face to face, and so are lost in worship and love. If, then we have truly loved them, if we have cared only for their highest happiness and their spiritual perfection, we shall be more than comforted concerning them, and we shall know that though they cannot come to us, when we will, we can go to them by the way of prayer and praise. Moreover, this practice of communion with the saints will be the best preparation for the final re-union, to which so many look forward as one of the richest rewards of death, and for their welcome home to the heavenly land. For it must be remembered that some preparation for that will be necessary, since it will not be a resumption of earthly relationships: " they neither marry nor are given in marriage, but they are as the angels "; though the negative side of this declaration must not obscure its welcome positive assurance. Too often earthly relationships are not only imperfect and a hindrance to spiritual advancement, they are sometimes so burdensome that their cessation is not only looked forward to, but anticipated. There must be many persons to whom the promise that heaven will restore them to their families and relations would seem a doubtful advantage, if not a dreadful prospect. But it must be remembered that the spirits of the blest in heaven will be purified of everything that here may have made them imperfect or unlovable, and we ourselves shall not enter heaven until we have passed through a similar process. We shall all be changed, but the change will leave us still our individual, identifiable selves, though infinitely more delightful and attractive. The real personality will survive, purged of defects and disabilities, and with all its spiritual potentialities reached and realized. It will be the spiritual affinities, and not mere ties of kinship, or bonds of blood, that will draw and hold us together; and this because all souls will be seen in God, and

OUR RELATIONSHIP WITH THE DEPARTED

all relationships between them will be sanctified through union with Him.

Intercourse with the departed is to be regarded as governed by the same conditions as our communion with God. That is attained mainly through prayer, and although it is entirely spiritual, those who have attained to mystical prayer testify that it is so satisfying that nothing more can be imagined or desired. It is in communion with God that the communion of saints becomes a reality, and the communion of saints is intended to deepen and centre everything upon communion with God. These act and re-act upon one another, so that often where bereavement has broken in upon a love which has been of a high and unselfish order, and where faith is clear and strong, it may prove a means of drawing the soul much nearer God, and making the heavenly life seem much more desirable and real, thus establishing a relationship intimate and sacred, free from the passions which often entangle and the imperfections which always disappoint, and yet far more satisfying and sanctifying than even the highest love earth can hold.

This spiritual relationship with the departed not only awakens the soul more strongly to God, and solves all problems of personality by centring everything in Him, but does not selfishly or narrowly centre our interest in the departed upon one soul, but gives us an introduction to the whole company of heaven. It prepares us for a wide and wealthy relationship with all souls departed this life; and will help us to feel ourselves at once at home among the society of the redeemed, and in the communion of saints see reflected, and thus discern more fully, the grace and glory of God.

XI

THE PAROUSIA

THE Parousia may be an unknown term to some, but it is for that very reason a more convenient title than such terms as the Second Coming or the Last Advent; for it is their Greek equivalent in the New Testament, and its very unfamiliarity will serve to remind us that this is a subject on which the popular mind is confused by sectarian speculations; which nevertheless remains, despite the researches of modern scholarship, in considerable obscurity; and is probably intended by divine providence to lie beyond certain knowledge or clear interpretation. The Parousia simply means " the Presence " of the Lord; and that of itself indicates that it may be capable of different manifestations: a presence realized within the heart, a presence gradually made manifest to the world, a presence suddenly precipitated and revealed to all.

Over and over again in our Gospels, as firmly taught in the Epistles, and depicted in flaming colours in the Apocalypse, the return of Jesus Christ to this earth is unmistakably predicted. In the Acts of the Apostles it is declared that Christ's return will be after the same manner as His Ascension; in the Gospels it is often referred to as the coming in glory of the Son of man; and St. Paul describes it in memorable language: " The Lord Himself shall descend from heaven, with a shout, with the voice of the archangel, and with the trump of God: and the dead in Christ shall rise first;

then we that are alive, that are left, shall together with them be caught up in the clouds to meet the Lord in the air." Language could not more clearly express the visibility, the supernatural character, and the stupendous nature of this event. It has naturally awakened vivid expectation or fearful apprehension, and given rise to many curious speculations as to when it is likely to occur. The general opinion of Christendom has been that this Second Coming will inaugurate the Last Judgment, and will not therefore occur until the end of the world; this, it is then too often hastily concluded, we can safely assume to be remote, especially as it will be heralded by unmistakable signs that the end of history is approaching; and of this there is no evidence visible or as yet to be expected. On the other hand, it is known that the early Christians believed even in their time that Christ's return was imminent; and indeed this was clearly taught by St. Paul, though he had to contradict false expectations that it was to take place immediately; and its nearness seems to have been even more definitely announced by our Lord Himself. Impatience, or even loss of faith due to the delay, had to be rebuked, and the delay explained, even in New Testament times. As centuries passed, hopes of a speedy fulfilment faded away, to revive, however, at any outbreak of physical catastrophe or political upheaval; expectation grew excited as the first thousand years of Christian history neared their consummation; and since the Reformation, especially in the closing decades of the nineteenth century, private interpretation of the Scriptures gave rise to novel beliefs, fantastic speculations and confident prediction, even highly detailed diagrams being constructed, giving a complete series of events, in some cases with the dates when they might be expected to occur.

The majority of Christians, whether Catholic or Protestant, have refused to be other than amused at what they regard as crude interpretations and fantastic literalism. The abundance and definiteness of the Scriptural material on which these speculations have been based, and to which such interpretations confidently appeal, demand, however, more consideration. By modern scholarship, the language of Scripture describing Christ's Second Coming has been either interpreted as a highly coloured symbolism of purely spiritual events, or, by the more radical school, referred to apocalyptic notions inherited from current Jewish ideas; these ideas were doubtless shared by the Apostle Paul, and perhaps by the Twelve; thus leading to the misunderstanding of Christ's teaching, or even to extensive interpolations in the Gospels. Catholic interpretation and conventional opinion have generally concurred in discouraging all speculation on the subject as expressly forbidden by Scripture; if a literal fulfilment is still to be looked for, as Catholic opinion generally holds, this is of no immediate concern; and the whole idea is replaced among enlightened Protestants by the expectation of a future for human history, perhaps as vast as the antiquity which research and science now demand, or the subject is dismissed as a piece of mythology which Christianity has now outgrown; if it is traceable to Christ's teaching, then it must be regarded as a limitation of His outlook, due to His sharing the mentality of His contemporaries, and of no more scientific value than His belief in demon possession.

Catholic theology does not take kindly to the idea of interpolations in the original text, to misunderstanding on the part of the Evangelists, or to any limitation on the part of Christ's mind which would involve erroneous notions and misleading expectations. Catholic theology may consequently find itself faced with serious critical and historical difficulties; but it at least avoids the too easy device of removing suspected interpolations, often with no more sanction than subjective dislike; while the endeavour to maintain that our Lord, in His human mind, or within the purview of His earthly mission, may not have known certain things, such as the very day and hour of His return, and yet could have taught no error nor been under any delusion, does have the advantage of demanding more patient consideration of His teaching and of truths the Gospels may contain. In addition, modern radical criticism on this subject has gone through a complete revolution, and instead of regarding the eschatological elements in the Gospels as interpolations, or Christ's apocalyptic outlook as a mental limitation which can be ignored, it now regards these elements as authentic and the apocalyptic idea as the dominant colouring of His mind, and the surest clue to His meaning. The imminence of His coming in glory was Christ's confident expectation, and the very core of His conception of the kingdom; this was to be established, neither by the slow spread of the faith, nor by a gradual evolution, not even through human co-operation, but by a sudden irruption of the spiritual realm into this present order. The Apocalyptic school of interpretation has had considerable influence, since it does do justice to indisputable elements in the Gospels; nevertheless, it would not for a moment sanction the crude expectations of the literalist sects. It evades such a sanction because this teaching it regards as merely symbolic of man's entire dependence upon God, and of the constant possibility of the coming of His kingdom if there were only faith to believe it and the will to establish it; or else, while ruthlessly demanding the admission that on this issue Christ shared the literal expectations which misled many of His followers, it is held that they have been so discredited by the course of history that no deferred fulfilment of them is now to be expected. It is difficult to see what reliance upon the rest of Christ's teaching, or how the most reduced idea of the Incarnation could be retained, if the more radical interpretation of Christ's apocalyptic teaching had to be accepted; but there are already signs that it is failing to win general acceptance among scholars.

If Catholic opinion is to be of any help in clearing up this confusion, and is to maintain itself against sceptical conclusions, it has to throw light upon, and find a synthesis for, three sets of not easily reconcilable facts. First of all, it must do justice to the explicit declarations and the general sense of the imminence of Christ's return, which the Gospels undoubtedly convey, thereby meeting the facts stressed by the apocalyptic school of criticism, as well as satisfying that watchful expectancy, which, although it has often been left to the literalist to keep alive, is indisputably the reiterated conclusion of all Christ's teaching on this subject. Secondly, it must do justice to the other schools of interpretation, which have stressed the equally indubitable references to slow growth and extended outlook demanded for the propagation of the Gospel and the establishment of the Church. Thirdly, it must relate the ending of human history to an act of God which can be shown to be in accordance with His general dealings with mankind, be consistent with the spiritual principles of our Lord's teaching, and, whatever delay may take place, perfectly fulfil all Christ's promises concerning His return in glory.

It would be well if we were first to clear up a fruitful source of misunderstanding, namely, the idea of the Millennium. Some early Christians held the belief that Christ would return to earth in order to set up a visible kingdom which should last for a thousand years. This idea has frequently been revived in modern literalist speculation, sometimes combined with the belief that, before this reign of Christ and His saints is established, there will take place a secret return of Christ to gather His elect to Himself. Only after the thousand years are fulfilled, and a rebellion of satanic forces has broken out, will Christ's final advent to Judgment take place. There has been no explicit condemnation of such beliefs by Catholic authority, but the general tendency of Catholic opinion is to identify the Millennium with the reign of the Church, the thousand years being only symbolical of a perfectly fulfilled period; and this interpretation evades the considerable ethical difficulties which burden the conception of a literal Millennium, and is therefore safer to follow, especially since the conception has such slight and doubtful basis in Scripture.

We are now left to face the apparently clear promise of an early return of Christ in glory and its equally apparent disappointment. Some modern expositors are inclined to favour the idea that this prediction falls under the general law, which can be discerned as governing scriptural prophecy, namely, that Christ, like the Old Testament prophets, by a kind of foreshortened vision, due to its vivid clearness, predicted as imminent, as from the divine

THE PAROUSIA

outlook it would be, that which might only take place after the passage of what, according to human calculation, might be vast ages of time. The sanction for such an interpretation is sought in the text, "one day is with the Lord as a thousand years and a thousand years as one day." Others have regarded our Lord's predictions as, also like some Old Testament prophecies, being dependent upon contingent events, such as the fidelity of His Church, or the repentance of mankind. While bringing a certain relief to obvious difficulties, these interpretations leave the whole subject very vague, and the details either meaningless or hopelessly obscure. It will no doubt be widely felt that the promises of an imminent return cannot be so easily explained away. It would therefore be well to examine in more detail what those promises actually were.

Just after the confession of St. Peter, our Lord is reported by St. Mark to have said, "There be some here of them that stand by, which shall in no wise taste of death, till they see the kingdom of God come with power"; or, as St. Matthew reports it, "till they see the Son of man coming in His kingdom"; or as in St. Luke, "till they see the kingdom of God." There is a vagueness about these statements which makes it possible to hold that, whether the kingdom of God is an interior experience, an external manifestation of justice and peace, or both, this prediction is sufficiently fulfilled by the outpouring of the Holy Spirit at Pentecost and the founding of the Church. We have another saying recorded by St. Matthew which declares, "Ye shall not have gone through the cities of Israel till the Son of man be come." It seems useless to try to stretch this saying to embrace the failure, even to the present time, to convert the Jews. The only alternative is to take the coming of the Son of man to refer to some event previous to the final advent of Christ. If other references are now examined this seems to be a not impossible interpretation. Our Gospels certainly contain an explicit prediction of the destruction of Jerusalem, and after that event, and, according to St. Matthew's report, *immediately* after it, "the Son of man shall be seen coming on the clouds of heaven with power and great glory." Now the destruction of Jerusalem did facilitate the further establishment of the Church, since it was thereafter no longer challenged by the continuation of the Old Testament Church. Can we then take the coming of the Son of man in glory to be a gradual event identifiable with the growth of the Church ? If we look at Christ's confession before Caiaphas, as recorded by St. Matthew: "henceforth ye shall see the Son of man sitting at the right hand of power, and coming on the clouds of heaven"; this seems to represent that coming as a process. If we may envisage that process as punctuated by the great crises in human history, in which kingdoms are overthrown, the Church comes to greater power, or a further opportunity of establishing the kingdom of God is given ; if we can regard these crises as working up to a decisive issue and glorious consummation in the Last Advent ; and if we keep in mind the variety of Christ's references to His return, some as imminent and some to be delayed, and depending upon such signs as the proclamation of the Gospel to the whole world, or the onset of such tribulations as shall imperil the existence of faith, not all of which can be easily reconciled with the idea of a single coming, after a single fashion; then we do seem to be in possession of an interpretation that covers all the relevant facts and embraces apparently divergent predictions.

This interpretation of Christ's coming again as a process, developing through crises to a consummation, seems to be expressly sanctioned by the Fourth Evangelist. Radical critics have suspected this author of deliberately spiritualizing the expectation of a Second Advent; for he expressly identifies Christ's coming again with His reception by the soul, with the outpouring of the Holy Spirit, or again, with the coming of death to the individual. But that this is a legitimate interpretation can be confirmed from the Synoptic Gospels; and, moreover, the Fourth Gospel does not so spiritualize Christ's coming as to leave no place for a visible return, nor does the author abandon the idea of the Last Day, the Resurrection, or the Judgment as mere materialistic mythology; these are retained by the Evangelist, and still figure as the term of all earthly existence. Further, it should be noted that the Gospel references to Christ's return are made in two forms: first, it is illustrated by numerous parables, and that the parabolic form should be chosen is in itself an indication that we are dealing with realities more easily expressed in symbolic than in literal description; secondly, when He refers to His second coming more explicitly, it is always as the coming of the Son of man. Now Christ's name for Himself as the Son of man, and the references to the Son of man coming on the clouds of heaven, are reminiscent of the great vision in Daniel; and there, without doubt, the Son of man stands not for an individual only, but is the symbol of a humane kingdom. There can be no doubt whatever that our Lord identified Himself with the Son of man, but His preference for this term seems to demand that it means something more than a cumbrous circumlocution for " I." It seems rather to mean, on the one hand, " ideal humanity " as that is embodied in Christ, and, on the other, that humane kingdom which Christ was divinely ordained to establish, and of which He is head. The coming of the Son of man, the growth of the Church, and the establishment of the Kingdom are therefore in some degree interchangeable terms, as any interpretation of the New Testament as a whole certainly demands. Therefore in this idea of Christ's coming again we have in symbolic form a philosophy of history which interprets all human events, however long the world may last, as events which contain the possibility of a further manifestation of the kingdom of God and a revelation of the glory of Christ, leading up to a final event in which that kingdom will be established for ever and that glory perfectly revealed to all.

It only remains to be shown that this idea is true to human history, demands a constant spiritual vigil, and gives us the only rational hope of what shall be the goal of human history. Whether God's kingdom shall come on earth, and Christ become more manifest as history advances, depends upon the fidelity of His Church, and especially upon its power to seize the opportunity and interpret the great crises of history. Similar language to that in which Christ describes His return, such as its being heralded or accompanied by physical catastrophes, is employed by the Old Testament prophets to signify the downfall of kingdoms; and these are events which often offer an opportunty for the further establishment of a kingdom of righteousness and faith. Physical events like earthquakes, and human calamities like wars, again point the moral of the instability of man's earthly home and the insecurity of all secular affairs, and remind us that here we have no continuing city. It is true that in our own times this somewhat tragic reading of history has been replaced by the idea of a steady, comfortable, and inevitable evolution of humanity, extended over vast vistas of future time, and reaching some culmination of perfection beyond our vision or even our hopes. To such an interpretation the insistent expectation of Christ's coming again is a challenge, but it is a challenge which the Church ought not to be ashamed constantly to present. For, in the first place, there is little indication in history that human progress follows such an inevitable evolution. There is still an undecided battle being fought out on this globe between light and darkness, faith and unbelief, justice and tyranny. And the instability of society, threatened by the constant change of political experiment, the suicidal policy of a materialistic industrialism, and the recurring cataclysm of ever-intensified international strife, have to be set alongside the hopes of democratic emancipation, enlightened education and the scientific exploitation of natural power. Further, physical science gives us no assurance that this earth is destined to be a permanent home for the human race, nor even any assurance of a prolonged extension of humanity's career. As this earth has evolved to become a suitable dwelling-place for mortals, so it is likely to evolve into becoming an unsuitable one. There is no guarantee against our collision with some heavenly body that would dissolve the whole earth in fire and ashes; a wave in the ether might disintegrate every atom of matter that exists; human existence protracted to an indefinite period

THE PAROUSIA

would, by the mere multiplication of the species, exhaust earth's resources and make it uninhabitable. Now if we believe in a purpose for man which earthly life cannot embrace, and a divine Providence which overrules human history, the future of humanity cannot be left merely to the play of human forces, natural resources, or physical catastrophes. Not only in and through, but beyond and above them, God is working and keeping watch; and at any moment, it may be conceived, the end of human history may be determined, either because human history has served its purpose in the training of man for a heavenly life, or because humanity is in danger of losing its faith and finally perverting that purpose. When either of these events draws near, we may look for a divine intervention more stupendous and staggering than anything hitherto known or able to be conceived. And just as the First Coming of Christ fulfilled the Old Testament prophecies, first, in a spiritual way that prophecy itself came to demand, and secondly, by combining what, before the Incarnation, looked like irreconcilable expectations, so we may expect that Christ's Second Coming will fulfil all the New Testament prophecies in a way we shall probably never be able to conceive until that event arrives.

It is, of course, impossible for us to picture beforehand that dreadful event, which shall at once dissolve the material universe, summon every soul into the presence of God, and reveal the secrets of all hearts; neither can we imagine what will be entailed in our being suddenly confronted with the realities of the spiritual world, in the creation of a new heaven and a new earth, or in being clothed with a spiritual body. But unless we can hope for some such consummation of earthly existence and human history, we seem to be faced with the alternatives of an everlasting progress to some infinite goal which can never be attained, and therefore to something in itself meaningless and unsatisfying, or with the gradual decay of the material universe and the decline of the human race in fear, loneliness and agony. The idea of the need for some such divine intervention is neither unscientific nor unhistorical; there was at least such an intervention at the Creation, there was certainly another at the Incarnation, and there will have to be a third to fulfil the purpose of both.

This hope does not, however, come under the same objection which has often been raised against the notion of the Millennium, namely, that coercive forces have to be applied to human affairs in order to establish the kingdom of God; for since the Millennium is supposed to give way to a further outbreak of evil, it must have involved some form of repression, and be therefore without religious value. It would, indeed, then seem as if, having begun in the spirit, we were to be perfected in the flesh; whereas, the kind of intervention involved in the Last Advent will not be undertaken in order to make men righteous by force, or good against their will. This distinction remains even if we allow that the hope of the Final Advent embraces two contingencies: the one that if humanity were to involve itself in irremediable misery God would intervene to save us from despair, or the other, if humanity progressed to a sufficient spirituality, then God would translate us all to a higher order of existence. An act of coercion may be useless for making men morally better; it may be quite effective for preventing them from destroying themselves. And the transference of human existence from one condition to another may necessitate a further intervention in any conceivable process of spiritual development, if the reward of eternal life is to crown the sufficient preparation for that which earthly life may have attained. Which of these two causes will condition Christ's Advent we cannot predict. He Himself asked the question whether, when the Son of man came, He would find the faith upon the earth; and it was a question to which He gave no answer. We can perhaps therefore assume that He would come in response to a sufficient faith, even as the Church has been taught to pray; but also that He would come if faith entirely disappeared, and then in order to save us from the intolerable consequences that would entail for earthly life. The New Testament appears to regard either of these contingencies as possible, and nowhere clearly or certainly declares which we are to expect. There will, we are promised, be signs of the end, but they may be signs in either direction, and they may not be easy to read. The complete acceptance of the Gospel by mankind, and with such application to all human life that the kingdoms of this world would be perfectly submitted to the rule of Christ, would be one of the signs of the imminence of the end, for the purpose of earthly existence would have been attained. The final rejection of the Gospel by mankind, accompanied by the reign of terror and despair that this would precipitate, would also be a sign that the last time had arrived. But no one of us can tell the conditions which God would regard as demanding the cessation of this present order of existence and the winding up of human history.

This general interpretation has, at least, this practical value, that it keeps alive that need for

THE PAROUSIA

incessant vigil which is the constant warning attached to all our Lord's predictions of His return; and therefore any conception of the Second Advent that makes it unnecessary to watch must be wrong, whatever other advantages it may claim; we can never say at any moment, This, at any rate, is not the time. For while our Lord Himself, in His incarnate humanity, knew not the day nor the hour, He has also told us that it will be at such a time when we think *not*; there will be an element of surprise in it for all, against which we shall do well to be forewarned. At any day, or at any hour, at midnight, at cockcrow, or at the dawn, all things may come to an end. And even if we ourselves may not live to endure the test that event will certainly impose on all, there is a spiritual coming of Christ which is repeated in every generation, and for which His Church is warned to watch, lest the opportunity pass and we be condemned for our unpreparedness. Further, there is a coming of our Lord which may be indeed at any moment, for which we all must be ready: His coming to call for us at the hour of our death; and therefore, for everyone, soon or late, there will be an event which is an anticipation of the Last Advent; for us all, at one moment or another, this world will be no more, judgment will have to be faced, and we must be ready to enter upon an entirely new order of existence where spiritual things alone are real. While, therefore, we cannot agree with those who claim that the whole of Christ's apocalytic teaching is only a highly-coloured symbolism for the irruption of death into the individual life, that, nevertheless, is a practical application of the need of vigil which all the teaching about the Second Advent enforces. But the higher and wider significance remains that

His Church must both watch and pray for His return; for the Church can never be content with earthly conditions, whatever they are, and the Church must never settle down with the assurance that there is plenty of time; the Church must always live under a crisis of expectancy, and in answer to His promise, "I come quickly," among its prayers there must ever be the petition, "Even so, come, Lord Jesus."

XII

THE FUTURE OF CHRISTIANITY

IT is entirely beyond the power of speculation to predict the future, immediate or final, of the Christian faith in this world of ours. Its collapse has often been prophesied by its enemies; the saints have often lamented its precarious condition; it has rarely wanted at its worst times those who looked for its revival. The ordinary Christian is probably convinced that the ultimate victory of the faith is the one assured fact of the future; to doubt it would be itself a denial of the faith, for surely this much has been already revealed. Yet if we turn to the revelation of the future contained in the Scriptures, careful examination will soon show that on this subject they seem to be obscure or ambiguous. It is indeed strange and interesting to note that, on the whole, the Old Testament speaks with a more optimistic note than the New. The Old Testament prophecies look forward to a time when the Law given to Israel shall be accepted by the whole world, which shall result in such an establishment of peace between the nations, that they shall beat their spears into ploughshares and learn war no more. Not only is it predicted that all Israel, from the least to the greatest, shall know the Lord, but it is declared that the earth shall be filled with the knowledge of the Lord, as the waters cover the seas. Similarly, in the New Testament we have our Lord's promise that the Church shall be built so firmly that the gates of hell shall not prevail against it. One

THE FUTURE OF CHRISTIANITY

parable depicts the growth of the kingdom, as from a mustard seed, until it becomes a great tree, providing shade and refuge; and another parable likens it to the leaven which, hidden in the meal, at last leavens the whole; and there is the definite prediction that the end of the world shall not come until the Gospel has been preached to all the nations. On the other hand, the New Testament foretells that in the last times there shall be a great increase of iniquity, rebellion and denial; the day of the Lord shall not come until the great apostasy has taken place; and our Lord Himself raised the question whether, when the Son of man came, He should find the faith upon the earth; which question He left unanswered one way or the other. The Book of the Revelation foresees the kingdoms of this world becoming the kingdom of Christ, and closes with the vision of the New Jerusalem coming down out of heaven to earth; but it is very doubtful whether this means the complete establishment of the heavenly kingdom in this present world; Christ's victory seems to take place only by the destruction of the kingdoms of this world. There has to take place the creation of a new heaven and a new earth; and elsewhere we find prophecies which seem to imply not only the overthrowing of the world order, but the destruction of the very fabric of the earth, and apparently the dissolution of the whole universe by fire.

A pessimistic outlook is sometimes adopted by Christians of very different schools and ecclesiastical attachment: Plymouth Brethren and Roman Catholics sometimes strangely agreeing in complete hopelessness concerning the conversion of all mankind to the Christian faith. Sometimes such

THE FUTURE OF CHRISTIANITY

expectations are used to discourage any hope of the establishment on earth of an order of social righteousness, as if it it were something inherently impossible, human nature and economic law being what they are; and where these expectations include a belief in the literal millennial reign of Christ on earth, this is regarded as both temporary and superficial, for it is only succeeded by a further outburst of wickedness and rebellion.

Some light on this obscure subject and a reconciliation of opposed methods could perhaps be found in the idea of divergent possibilities, and some sanction of this seems involved in the petition we have been taught by our Lord continually to offer : " Thy kingdom come, Thy will be done on earth as it is heaven." For that we are bidden to pray thus implies two things : first, that the perfect doing of the will of God on earth is possible ; secondly, that it is not inevitable ; for we should never pray for the impossible, and for the inevitable there is no need to pray. It would therefore appear that, taking the Scriptures as a whole, we are presented with an option : there is nothing inherently impossible in the full coming of the kingdom of God upon the earth ; and since this is inconceivable unless the great majority of people acknowledge the Christian faith, and the nations willingly accept Christ's reign, this shows that there is no inherent hindrance to the acceptance of the Christian faith by mankind, the gathering of the whole world into the Catholic Church, and the establishment on earth of a kingdom which perfectly embodies the will of God for humanity. If we then consider those predictions of the New Testament which apparently contradict the hope of these possibilities ever being realized, we can perhaps be

THE FUTURE OF CHRISTIANITY

allowed to apply the obvious law governing predictions of doom in the Old Testament, where it is always understood that they will be cancelled if men repent. Taking these differing outlooks, together with the general interpretation of the Parousia to which our previous examination has led, it seems safe to conclude that the future of Christianity is an entirely open question. There is no reason, either in the mind of man, or in the nature of Christianity, why it should not at last win perfect assent from every living soul; on the other hand, there is no guarantee that this will actually take place. The nature of the Parousia will be itself conditioned by the extent to which mankind accepts the Christian faith. If the Christian faith as a whole is accepted, and the kingdoms of this earth accept the sovereignty of God, there may be a growing manifestation of Christ and a transformation of earthly conditions, which could be described as heaven descending upon the earth. If there is such a final rejection of faith as to make further recovery hopeless, then this transformation will be effected by earth being, as it were, subsumed, though through dreadful catastrophe and suffering, into the heavenly order.

We are, therefore, left free to consider the present prospects and immediate future of Christianity, not with any idea of predicting the final issue, though bearing in mind that the final victory will be with God, whether with or without man's co-operation; and our concern being not so much the prediction of the future, but such a consideration of the possibilities as shall call the Church to a greater activity and compel all Christians to recognize their responsibility for the future of the faith.

The issue concerns the Church, and in part

THE FUTURE OF CHRISTIANITY

depends upon the Church's fidelity to its commission. We have Christ's promise that the gates of hell shall never prevail against the Church; but it is not perfectly clear what this promise implies. It is not said that the Church shall not prevail against the gates of hell, but only that the gates of hell shall not prevail against the Church. This may only mean that the powers of evil shall not utterly destroy the Church, or merely promises that the Church shall not be subject to the law of death which governs personal life, secular institutions, or national existence. This promise would therefore be fulfulled if the Church remained in existence, true to the faith, however small it might become. The Church was founded on one person at the beginning, and this promise would be fulfilled if there were found only one person faithful to the last, who, from any point of view, would be St. Peter's true successor. The wider world-issue is not entirely decided by the Church's fidelity, whether that be taken to involve merely the preservation and the proclamation of the one true faith in doctrinal form, or also the corresponding embodiment of that faith in a pure Church and a persuasive evangel. The absolute truth of Christianity gives no guarantee of its acceptance by mankind, which is often disposed to welcome anything but the truth; and even if the Church were faithful, not only in the preservation of pure doctrines, but in its perfect presentation to the understanding of every mind, especially if this were accompanied by a challenging witness on moral and social questions, that also would not guarantee that the Church's witness would be more welcome to the world, or its supremacy be the more easily acknowledged by the nations. It is quite possible that a Church perfectly faithful in every direction would incur such hostility from the world that its total destruction would be at least attempted. These considerations enable us to consider the present prospects of Christianity with a detachment that makes it possible to take an unbiassed and therefore a more probably accurate view. Our final hopes for the victory of God will not be imperilled by any immediate considerations; and whatever conclusion is forced upon us, nothing can diminish the demand for individual faithfulness, and the fulfilment of our commission, as if everything depended upon these alone, which in some degree it actually does.

If we took an external view of the history of Christian life and thought since the Reformation, it would be difficult to avoid the conclusion that, as a system of thought and as an ecclesiastical order, Christianity shows signs of breaking down. Outside the Roman system, which does not permit any departure from what has been authoritatively declared to be of faith, and outside its still maintained hierarchical order, there can be discerned a general movement towards the dissolution of faith and order. Whatever opinion be held about the Papacy, whether it is a divine appointment or a legitimate development, it would have to be admitted that outside submission to Rome, Christendom as a whole presents the appearance of a declining scale, in which all order is gradually abandoned, and any visible form of Church ceases to be discernible. First, papacy, then episcopacy, then priesthood, and then any regular ministry is repudiated, and refuge is taken at last in the idea of a Church which is so invisible that not only does it have no organization, but it never meets even for worship, the name "Christian" only standing for what is vaguely called sharing the spirit of Christ. It has to be considered that while each more radical departure from Catholic order still probably holds a correspondingly smaller following, there are those who maintain that, with the last disappearance of organization, Christianity will be freed from the inevitable corruption that all institutionalism involves, and it will then gradually spread through the world, not only in a purer, but in a much more permeating form. What the Catholic fears as a sign of disappearance, the anti-institutionalist welcomes as a sign of growth. It is to be noted, however, that with the diminution of Catholic order there goes also the dilution of Catholic doctrine. The decrease in the definiteness of order can be paralleled at every stage by a decrease in the definiteness of faith. Here, again, we must take note of the confident assumption on the part of some that this also is a great advantage: Christianity will be set free from the doctrinal shackles which have only hindered its acceptance and should never have been placed upon it. And with the recovery of the idea that Christianity is not a creed to be accepted by the mind, but a life to be lived, a following of Christ, whose loyalty is dictated solely by love for Him, it is believed that all that is essential to Christianity will be retained, and will the more quickly create an interior spiritual attitude and an external social order, corresponding to the kingdom of God which Christ proclaimed.

It has, however, to be pointed out that there is plenty of evidence that the Christian ethic is not going to live apart from Christian doctrine; it has been challenged in this generation as entirely dependent upon dogmatic sanctions, and, in itself, is neither morally attractive nor socially useful. Moreover, when the personality of Christ has been

THE FUTURE OF CHRISTIANITY

shorn of the doctrinal explanations which the Church has adopted, and deprived of the perpetual accessibility which the Sacraments provide, it has been found that He not only becomes vague, distant, and shadowy, but His worthiness or efficiency as an ideal to be followed are challenged. There is a movement in criticism which follows the same process of diminution that we have noticed in order and in doctrine; the idea of Christ being God and Man in one person is first denied: He becomes a man who in some not quite conceivable way is actually elevated to Godhead; then His Godhead is interpreted as a mere poetic apotheosis, as an expression of His supreme excellence and virtue. The doctrine of Christ's Godhead is retained, but only as a judgment of value, not as a predication; and naturally it soon comes to be questioned whether this value is not a purely human value, and therefore subjective and fictitious. And then, when Christ is regarded as a man who merely happens to be the highest human image of God the race has produced, questions soon begin to rise, how we know enough about God to know that Christ is His image, or whether we may not look for some more perfect image yet. Or, if the emphasis shifts to the idea that Christ was merely a teacher, who tells us the truth about God more clearly and perfectly than anyone else, the question again arises as to how He in particular knew the truth about God, or what guarantee we have that He knew any more about God than those who confess they know nothing. It is not long before another movement begins to show itself. Christ made claims, either directly or indirectly, that are so incompatible with mere humanity, that it must be concluded that He, at least, thought Himself to

THE FUTURE OF CHRISTIANITY

be divine; and if this is dismissed as untrue, then He must have been fundamentally deceived, in short, mentally insane, however sane He may have been on other subjects. If He fulfilled the prophecies of His death, it was so by plotting to bring about His own crucifixion; and so to insanity there is added suicide. Others profess to solve the problem another way, and totally deny that there was ever such a person as Jesus of Nazareth. The arguments brought against the sanity or the historical existence of Christ may be dismissed as the *reductio ad absurdum* of radical criticism; they certainly cannot both be true, and they both produce arguments for their position which cancel one another out. But however unsound the criticism and ridiculous the results, the general effect in the minds of many people is to produce the impression that no certainty is attainable as to who Jesus was, or what He taught, whether He was trustworthy or whether He actually existed; and therefore He can no longer be a living inspiration or a vital personality with whom anyone can now come into friendly or saving contact. The religion, therefore, which lives solely upon what it calls the spirit of Christ is very different from what is meant by the Spirit of Christ in the New Testament, and threatens to present us with something more like the ghost of Christ, ever more cloudy, doubtful, and ineffective.

There are, however, inveterate optimists who believe that while the collapse of Christianity is, in many respects, regrettable, it is inevitable, and we must turn to other faiths, which may do more for the future than Christianity has done for the past. They may first turn to pure Theism, which must rely less and less upon Christ, and so is forced to construct for itself either a theosophy by eclectic combination

THE FUTURE OF CHRISTIANITY

from other religions, or a spiritualistic philosophy. But it will be gradually discovered that all such systems are difficult to defend, because they rest upon so insecure a foundation, and they decline continually into pantheism, which at last is found to be only a poetic name for materialism, and is, in the end, indistinguishable from atheism. There are those who, while, unwilling to commit themselves to dogmatic atheism, regard all theological questions as beyond the power of the human mind to decide, and yet they are convinced that the law of progress will take humanity to such a height of knowledge and power that the physical, social and mental improvement of mankind can form a sufficient faith, ideal and concern for the individual human soul. It has, however, to be pointed out that no such law of inevitable progress is supported by history or philosophy. Moreover, the possibility of immediate progress is crossed by a threefold menace: the disaster of a further international conflict, against which humanity has still no guarantee; the still more inevitable and wasting strife between capital and labour; and man's interior mental conflict, which threatens to undermine his sanity. It is difficult to see how mankind is going to find its way past these three difficulties without the aid of faith; and even if it could, whether mankind could ever content itself with a merely earthly life, however insured against physical pain, and with the improvement of the social order, however just and frictionless it might be made. Science can promise us no permanent home for the human species on this earth; industrial civilization is compelled to destroy the resources on which it exists; the multiplication of the species must inevitably overtake the production of their sustenance, and the endeavour to limit

THE FUTURE OF CHRISTIANITY

the species by artificial means will have psychological, if not physical reactions of a disastrous kind.

There is another fact which needs to be considered: atheism is to-day being proclaimed, not so much as a conclusion to which scientific research and philosophical reflection have brought us, but as the only foundation for the social emancipation of humanity and the coming of a kingdom which, although it cannot be called the kingdom of God, will be all the more a kingdom of justice and humanity, because it has got rid of the conception of a Supreme and Sovereign Being. The gospel that is running through the earth at present is the gospel of a social order, absolutely just, but an order from which faith must be eliminated if it is to be established and sustained. Whether such an order is possible without a coercion which must destroy both justice and humanity, or would satisfy or indeed be long liked by anybody; whether life, however improved and insured, would be tolerable without personal faith, is certainly open to question. If it were finally understood and accepted by all that the idea of God is a delusion and phantasy of which the human mind must rid itself, it would soon be realized that truth itself had no basis in the human mind, and so all philosophy and even culture would at length be undermined. With the general acceptance of the conviction that personal life comes to an end at death, the substitutes of racial immortality or survival in memory would soon be worked through; and it would then be seen that personal life has no meaning, sanity would be imperilled, and the further existence of any person who happened to be incurable, burdensome, or in any way a hindrance, would be given the choice of voluntary or compulsory euthanasia; and the life that had been made everything would soon be worth very little. Such an existence, however externally perfect, would contain the seeds of its own destruction, social, personal or racial.

The future of humanity is therefore identical with the future of Christianity. Looking out upon the world to-day with eyes sharpened by the outlook that was Christ's, it is impossible to exaggerate the crisis between hope and despair that the modern situation presents. Never was there such need for the Church to proclaim the faith and make the Gospel known; if only first of all the Church could be united, and that Gospel could be made clear, not only as a theological doctrine, but in its application to all international, social and personal needs. As men understand, as they are soon bound to, where unbelief and negation are leading, they will be more willing to reconsider the Christian faith. We may expect, therefore, to see considerable reaction towards a dogmatic faith and a definite ecclesiasticism on the part of many; but mere panic will not find the secret of Christianity, or make it known to the world. Everything depends upon the power of the Church to unite itself again, to persuade mankind of its truth, and to become the guide and leader of the nations. In more than one parable our Lord set forth the critical nature of the responsibility that He committed to His followers, and no doctrine of the indefectibility of the Church must be allowed to diminish the need of vigilance, or to close our eyes to the fact that our Lord had to envisage the possibility of His servants being found unfaithful. This warning must therefore be applied to the Church, whosoever claims to be the Church. If, in the parable in which there is given to all the servants their authority and work, and a special commission is given to the porter to watch, that porter is to be identified with the ministry, the episcopacy or the papacy, then the command to watch comes to them at this hour with special force. In another parable Christ compares the household of faith to an establishment where it has been left to one of the servants to feed the rest. If this again is claimed to be the special prerogative of the Papacy, then to it the warning of the parable must be specially addressed, lest, if Christ's coming be delayed, and that servant should ill-treat his fellows and set an example of luxurious and profligate living, He will return unexpectedly and give that servant his portion with the hypocrites and the unbelieving. No one would claim that this warning has never been necessary in the history of the Papacy. But, if any Church is disposed, at this moment, to claim that it possesses superior light, the same parable goes on to give a warning that that Church had better apply to itself, namely: that the greater knowledge of God's will must only involve the greater punishment if there has been neglect and unfaithfulness. Whatever judgments are coming upon the world, the Church cannot be content with complacently proclaiming them, for the time has come when judgment must begin at the House of God.

The whole issue of the future therefore hangs upon the Church, and the heavier wherever it is claimed that the true Church is to be found. If the Church of Rome claims that for itself, then to that Church the warning is addressed. Very few can doubt that at this juncture the Church of Rome does hold the key to the situation; will the key be used to open the door to the future, or to close it against the hope of humanity? Much will depend first upon whether the Church of Rome will undertake the reunion of Christendom with more faith, hope and charity than is found amongst some sections of that communion. The ecclesiastical confusion of the other Churches, the grave defects of faith and order which they present, seem to fill some members of the Roman Church with despair. There seems to be little comprehension how much that confusion and unbelief have been due to their own action in the past; neither is it understood how Catholic doctrine has been misrepresented to Christian people, who would welcome the truth, if only the great system of theology, of which the Roman Church is the custodian, could be more clearly and patiently presented. The attitude of mind which regards the Reformation as due to nothing but human rebellion and wickedness needs to be replaced by the recognition that, if the Reformation had one traceable cause, that cause was in the Roman Catholic Church itself. And while all would admit that much has been done to reform and cleanse that Church, much still remains to be done, which alone keeps up the persistent protest of Protestantism. If the claim to be the one true Church could be so enunciated that it did not brand all other Churches as mere imitations, wilfully schismatic bodies, and dead branches of the true vine, but rather as brethren whose separation was due to misunderstandings on both sides, the cause of reunion would be hastened, and the hope of inclusion in one Church again might be near and hold out a wide embrace.

Further, if only the Catholic Church could recognize that much in modern thought, social aspiration and the desire for international peace are gropings after the light, which would have been all the easier seen if Rome had only been herself more faithful upon these issues, then she would not be content contemptuously to condemn, but rather patiently to show the rest of the truth that men needed to accept.

But even if the Church does not rise to the situation and, as a result, humanity turns permanently in a wrong direction, and the whole human situation is threatened with despair, we can still believe that God will never leave Himself without a witness, and it may be at the midnight hour of darkness that Christ will be manifested in glory, and the earthly career of humanity will be brought to its judgment. That manifestation will reveal to the unshepherded multitudes, who still dwell in darkness, the true light of the world, which they will then hail with joy. And those who have only known Christ as misrepresented to them by the careless teaching of His stewards, or by the inconsistent lives of His followers, will then see Him as He is, and will turn to Him in love and worship. The Church triumphant, which has been growing all down the ages, will then be replenished by all those who were faithful to the light they possessed; whereas to those who have had the light, but have been unfaithful to it, by keeping it to themselves in pride and exclusiveness, or have let it be obscured by their carelessness and inconsistency, the Day of the Lord will be a day of darkness and not of light.

Whatever be the final issue, beyond all earthly failure and human infidelity, there remains the heavenly triumph and the faithfulness of God. If the truth is rejected here, it will have to be faced elsewhere and admitted by everyone. If the cause of Christ is defeated on earth, it shall have its triumph in heaven; God has other worlds than this,

THE FUTURE OF CHRISTIANITY

and His ultimate victory is assured; His kingdom will alone remain, and the final issue is in His hands. It is for us to choose whether we shall be fellow-workers with Him, share in His triumph, and win the crown of those who endure to the end, and so hear His greeting: "Well done, good and faithful servant, enter thou into the joy of thy Lord."

INDEX

Abelard on the Atonement, ii, 184 ; 186
Adoptionism, ii, 153, 164
Agnosticism, Ch. II ; i, 17-32
Angels, Existence of, i, 62
Annals of Tacitus, ii, 37
Annihilationism, iv, 115 f.
Anselm, St., on the Atonement, ii ,183 ; 186
Apocalypse and Bestial Order, i, 124
Apollinarianism, ii, 155
Apostolic Christology, Ch. IX ; ii, 129-144
Aquinas, St. Thomas, on the Atonement, ii, 183
Ariston, ii, 109
Arminianism and Salvation, iv, 130
Athanasius, St., ii, 160
Atheism, i, 17 ff.
   and Social Emancipation, iv, 187
Atonement, the, Ch. XII ; ii, 177-196 ; i, 95 ; ii, 85 f. ; 156 ; iii, 124
   and Purgatory, iv, 83 f.
Augustine, St., on the Atonement, ii, 183
   on Christians outside the Church, iii, 48
   and the Donatists, iii, 86
   on Miracles, i, 154
   on Problem of Evil, i, 115
   on the Trinity, iii, 6
Authority, Ch. VI ; iii, 81-96

Baptism into Threefold Name, ii, 175 ; iii, 97
   Sacrament of, iii, 107-112
   of the Holy Ghost, iii, 8
   of Jesus, and the Trinity, iii, 3
   Christ's, iii, 134
Benediction, the Rite of, iii, 141
Bergson's " Creative Evolution," i, 71
Body, Soul, and Spirit, Ch. II ; iv, 17-32
Brahman, i, 185
Buddha, Virgin Birth of, ii, 121
Buddhism, i, 185 ; 188 ; 190 ; ii, 13

Calvinism and Soul's Destiny, iv, 129 f.
Canonization of Saints, iv, 150 f.
Capital Penalty, Is it right to inflict ? iii, 173
Catherine of Genoa, St., on Purgatory, iv, 90-96

INDEX

Catholic v. Reformed Churches, iii, 60
Ceremonial Worship, Principles of, iii, 136–138
    Is it necessary ? iii, 138–141
Cerinthianism, ii, 153
Christ, Baptism of, iii, 134
    Consciousness of, Ch. II ; ii, 65–80
    of the Creeds, Ch. X ; ii, 145–160
    Death of, Ch. VI ; ii, 81–96 ; 178
    Gospel Portrait of, Ch. II ; 17–32
    Healing Miracles and Modern Mental Therapeutics, ii, 158 f.
    our Judge, iv, 72–78
    Preparation for, Ch. I ; ii, 1–16
    Spirit of, as a Church basis, iv, 183 ff.
    Teaching of, Ch. IV ; ii, 49–64
    Crucified, Soul's Vision of, at Death, iv, 73 f.
    (see also under Jesus)
Christianity, Future of, Ch. XII ; iii, 177–192
    a Historical Religion, i, 188
    and Knowledge of God, i, 31 f.
    in Annals of Tacitus, References to, ii, 37
    Meeting Place of Providence and Grace, i, 110 f.
    and World Religions, i, 103
    Christian Science, iv, 8
Church, the Apostolic, Ch. II ; iii, 17–32 ; 49
    the Catholic, Ch. III ; 33–48 ; 49 f. ; 52 f. ; 55 f. ; 62
    the Holiness of the, Ch. IV ; iii, 49–64
    the Holy Spirit and the, Ch. I ; iii, 1–16 ; 18 f. ; 23 ff.
    and Humanity, Ch. XII ; iii, 177–192
    and Internationalism, Ch. XI ; iii, 161–176.
    New Testament idea of, iii, 4 ff.
    Protestant Conception of, iii, 51
    and the Social Order, Ch. X ; iii, 145–160
    the Unity of the, Ch. V; iii, 65–80
    on it depends the Future, iv, 189–191
Clement of Alexandria, St., on the Catholic Church, iii, 35
    of Rome, iii, 20 ; 22
Codex Sinaiticus and Birth of Jesus, ii, 118
Communion of Saints, Neglect of Doctrine by Protestantism, iv, 147
Comparative Religion, Ch. XII ; i, 177–192
    and Preparation for Christ, ii, 3
Consubstantiation, iii, 115
Creation, Ch. IV ; 49–64
    and Christian Philosophy, i, 71
    and Providence, i, 97 ; 100
Creed, Apostles', iii, 33 f. ; 50
    Athanasian, Christological Articles in, ii, 145 ; 157
    Athanasian, and Soul of Christ, iv, 23
    Athanasian, and the Trinity, ii, 161 f.; 167 ff.
    Nicene, iii, 17 ; 33

INDEX

Creed and Church Unity, iii, 73 f.
  its Foundation, iii, 84
  Agreement concerning, iii, 96
  and the Atonement, ii, 188
  and Christ's Death, ii, 85 f.
  the Christ of the, Ch. X ; ii, 145–160
  in the Churches, iii, 84
Criticism and Consciousness of Christ, ii, 65
  and Credibility of Gospels, ii, 33–46
  and Gospel Portrait of Christ, ii, 22–30
  and Historical Gospels, ii, 39
Cross of Christ, its Effect, ii, 190–193
Crucifixion in Relation to the Resurrection, ii, 82 ; 98 f.
Cyril of Jerusalem, St., on the Catholic Church, iii, 35
  of Alexandria, iii, 156

Dale, Dr., on Christ's Gospel, ii, 53
Dante on Church and State, iii, 164
Death and Resurrection, Ch. IV ; iv, 49–64
  and Christ's Resurrection Body, iv, 63
Deification, iv, 106
Demonic Powers, their Agency in the World, i, 123 f.
  Christ's Belief in, i, 123
Departed, our Relationships with the, Ch. X ; iv, 145–160
Destiny, What determines, Ch. IX ; iv, 129–144
Determinism, i, 85 seq.
Didache, the, iii, 22
Docetism, ii, 131 ; 152 f.
Donatists, iii, 36
Duns Scotus on the Atonement, ii, 186

Ebionism, ii, 152
Ectoplasm, ii, 106
Emanation Theory, i, 54 f.
Enhypostatic, ii, 158
Episcopacy in Early Church, iii, 20–23 ; 25 f. ; 49
Eucharist, the, Ch. VIII ; iii, 113–128
  and the Atonement, ii, 179
  Celebration of, iii, 82
  in Early Church, iii, 21 ; 23
  Christ's intention concerning, iii, 136
  Christ's institution of, ii, 28 ; iii, 98
  Justin Martyr on, iii, 21
  and Pagan Mysteries, i, 191
Eucharistic Vestments, iii, 137 f.
Eusebius and Baptismal Formula, ii, 165
Eutychianism, ii, 156
Evil, the Problem of, Ch. VIII ; i, 113–128
  and Christian Science, iv, 9
Evolution, and the Fall, Ch. V ; i, 65–80 ; 82

INDEX

Evolution and Evil, i, 120 f.
   and Material World, iv, 12 f.

Faith, iii, 88
   Evil, a Hindrance to, i, 113 ; 118 f. ; 128
   Saving, iv, 135 f.
   and Sanctifying Grace, iv, 134
Fall, Evolution and the, Ch. V ; i, 68–80
   and Animal Creation, i, 124
   and Cause of Evil in World, i, 120 ; 122
   and Human Freedom, i, 84 f. ; 87 ; 89 ; 94 f.
   and Man's Relation to the Physical Order, i, 147
   and Providence, i, 101
   and Soul's Continuance, iv, 51
Filioque Clause in Nicene Creed, iii, 41
   Doctrine of the, iii, 4
"Foundation Pillars" in the Gospels, ii, 42

Gnostics, their Psychology, iv, 20
   and Tertullian, iii, 20
Gnosticism, ii, 168
God, the Existence of, Ch. I ; i, 1–16 ; 36
   the Existence of, confirmed by the Incarnation, i, 32
   Can Man Know, Ch. II ; i, 17–32 ; iii, 90
   Christ's Teaching on, ii, 58 f.
   Consciousness of, in Old Testament, ii, 67
   and Evil, Ch. VIII ; i, 113–128
   Hebrew Conception of, ii, 7 f.
   and Miracles, Ch. X ; i, 145–160
   the Nature of, Ch. III ; i, 33–48 ; 53
   Omnipotence of, i, 114
   and Prayer, Ch. IX ; i, 129–144
   His Relation to Matter and the Human Mind, i, 53 f.
Gospel Portrait of Christ, the, Ch. II ; 17–32
Gospels, the Credibility of the, Ch. III ; ii, 33–48
   Date of, ii, 19
   Difficulties concerning the, ii, 20 f.
Grace, Ch. VII ; i, 97–112 ; iii, 98–100
   defined, i, 106–110
   and Human Freedom, iv, 134 ff.
Gravitation, i, 154 f.
Greek Mysteries, i, 186 f.
   Myths, i, 183

Heaven, Ch. VII ; iv, 97–112
   not missed through Ignorance, iv, 140
   and the Unbaptized, iv, 126 f.
Hell, Ch. VIII ; iv, 113–128 ; iv, 97 ; 99
Hinduism, i, 185 ; ii, 3 ; 13
Holy Ghost, the Baptism of the, iii, 8

INDEX

Holy Orders, iii, 105–107
Holy Spirit, the, and the Church, Ch. I ; iii, 1–16
    and the Trinity, ii, 163 seq.
Homoiousion, ii, 158
Homo-ousion, ii, 151 ; 154
Human Freedom and Responsibility, Ch. VI ; i, 81–96
    and Destiny, iv, 135
    and Sin, i, 126
Humanity, its Future identical with that of Christianity, iv, 188 f.
Hume on Cause and Effect, i, 150
    and the Ego, i, 2
    on Evidence for Miracles, i, 149
Huxley on Agnosticism, i, 120

Idealism, i, 51 ; iv, 6–8
Ignatius, St., on Apostolic Succession, iii, 21
    on the Catholic Church, iii, 34 f.
Immaculate Conception, the, ii, 115 ; 122 f. ; iii, 41
Immortality, Ch. III ; iv, 33–48
    of Man's Spirit, i, 6
    of the Race, i, 6
    without God, i, 6 f.
Impanation, Theory of, iii, 123 f.
Incarnation, the, and Buddhism, i, 190
    and the Cross, i, 101
    and the Fall, i, 101
    and God, i, 37
    and the Trinity, ii, 174
    and the Virgin Birth, ii, 114 f.
    Church bound to decide True Theory of, ii, 178
    Its Extension in the Church, iii, 16
    Historic Preparation for, i, 110
    Need of, on Agnostic Principles, i, 31 f.
Intercession, i, 137 ff.
Irenæus, St., on Apostolic Succession, iii, 21

Jerome, St., on Arianism, ii, 149
    on the Episcopate, iii, 25 f.
Jesus, the Death of, Ch. VI ; ii, 81–96
    the Spirit of, iii, 2
    the Teaching of, Ch. IV ; ii, 49–64
    (*see also under* Christ)
Josephus, Silence concerning Christ, ii, 37
Judgment, Ch. V ; iv, 65–80
    and Christ's Second Coming, iv, 162
Justin Martyr, iii, 21

Knowledge, different kinds of, i, 24 ; 28
Krishna, i, 185 ; 190

INDEX

Last Supper, the, and the Atonement, ii, 177
   and High Mass, iii, 137
   a Symbolic Rite, iii, 135
Liturgical Prayer, iii, 142–144
Logos, the, ii, 139 ; 141 ; 155 ; 158 ; 173 f.
Lord's Prayer, the, ii, 73 f ; iii, 142
Lourdes, i, 156

Maitreya, i, 186
Marcion and Old Testament, ii, 2
Mass, the, and the Atonement, ii, 179 ; 193 f. ; 196 ; iii, 124
   High, and Resemblance to Last Supper, iii, 137
   its Ritual and Ceremonial an Aid to Prayer, iii, 142 f.
   and Souls in Purgatory, iv, 153 ff.
   fuller Understanding of, needed, iii, 80
   (*see also under* Eucharist), iii, 113–128
Materialism, i, 51 ; iv, 4 ; 36
Matter, whence derived, i, 4
Metousiosis, iii, 125
Mind, i, 5 f ; 164 f. ; iv, 24
   and Matter, i, 52
Miracles, Ch. X ; i, 145–160
Mithraism and Christianity, ii, 14
   and the Christian Sacrament, i, 187
Monophysitism, ii, 156 f.
Montanism, iii, 12 ; 21
Motion, i, 4
Myers, F. W., and Christ's Resurrection, ii, 106

Nestorianism, ii, 124 ; 155 f.
Newman, the *Dream of Gerontius*, iv, 88 f.
Nirvana, i, 186

Organization in Ecclesiastical Affairs, iii, 3 ; 15 f.
Origen on Hell, iv, 116 f.

Pacifism, iii, 168–170
Pagan Mysteries and Christianity, iii, 121 f.
Pain, i, 115 f. ; 118 f. ; 120
Pantheism, i, 51
Papal Infallibility and Supremacy, iii, 41 ; 48 ; 79 f. ; 94 f.
Parousia, the, Ch. XI ; 161–176 ; 180
Passover, its Ceremonial, iii, 137
Paul's, St., Psychology, iv, 20–24
Penance, the Sacrament of, iii, 103 ff.
Peter's Confession, St., ii, 31 ; 69 ; 87
Petrine Supremacy, iii, 4 f. ; 31 ; 40 ; 48 ; 50
Philo, ii, 14
Pius IX and the Immaculate Conception, ii, 115

INDEX

Plato, ii, 15
Polycarp, St., ii, 47 ; iii, 20 ff. ; 27
Positivism and Comparative Religion, i, 184
Prayer, its Difficulties, Ch. IX ; i, 129–144
   Christ's Recognition of Need of Form in, iii, 142
   Christ and Repetitionary, iii, 143
   and Invocation of Saints, iv, 148–152
   and Intercession for Souls in Purgatory, iv, 152–155
   for the Coming of the Kingdom of God, iv, 179
Protestantism and Doctrine of Purgatory, iv, 84 f.
Providence and Grace, Ch. VII ; i, 97–112
Psycho-Analysis on Fear of Death, iv, 55 ff.
Psychology, Modern, and Comparative Religion, i, 177 f.
   and the Consciousness of Christ, ii, 77 f.
   and the Religious Instinct, i, 164
Purgatory, Ch. VI ; iv, 81–96 ; iv, 102
   Council of Trent on, iv, 81 ; 87 ; 153

Reason substituted for God, i, 8
   and Revelation, i, 56 f.
   and the Scepticism of the Instrument, iii, 93
Redemption and the Fall, i, 76 ; 79 f. ; 101
   and Human Freedom, i, 95
Reformation, Causes of, iii, 52 f ; iv, 190 ff.
   its Effects, iii, 55
Religion, Christ's Teaching about, ii, 59 f.
   a Definition of, i, 132
   the Instinct for, Ch. XI ; i, 161–176
Reserved Sacrament, the, iii, 115
Resurrection, the, Ch. VII ; ii, 97–112 ; 113 ; iv, 62 f.
   in Relation to the Crucifixion, ii, 82
   and Death, Ch. IV ; iv, 49–64
   the General, and Judgment, iv, 69 f.
   Reformation Thought on, iv, 70 f.
Ritual, Ch. IX ; iii, 129–144
   and Earliest Religion, i, 182 f.

Sabellianism, ii, 167
Sacrament, the, and Mithraism, i, 187
Sacramental System, the, Ch. VII ; iii, 97–112.
   and Comparative Religion, iii, 121
Scriptures, their Inerrancy, iii, 95
Second Advent (*see* the Parousia)
Sin, Ch V ; i, 90 seq.
   and Death, iv, 51
   and Evil, i, 121
   and Human Freedom, i, 126 f.
   Teaching of Jesus on, ii, 60 f.
   and Judgment, iv, 79 ;
   Memory of, after Death, iv, 76 f.

INDEX

Soul, the, Ch. II ; iv, 17–32 ; i, 39
  its Awakening, iv, 14–16
  in Christianity, iv, 37
  at Death, iv, 52 ; 55
  its Dependence upon God, i, 129 f.
  its Destiny (see Ch. IX) ; iv, 129–144
  in Eastern Thought, iv, 36
  in Greek Thought, iv, 34 f.
  in Hebrew Thought, iv, 35 f.
  the Satisfaction of, in Heaven, iv, 107.
Souls in Purgatory, Intercession for, iv, 152 f.
Spencer on Agnosticism, i, 20–23
Spiritualism and Communion with Departed Souls, iv, 145 seq.
  and the Resurrection, ii, 106 f.
  and the Soul's Immortality, iv, 36 ; 39 seq.
Suffering (see Evil, Problem of)
Suffering Servant, ii, 11 ; 13 ; 30 ; 72 ; 86
Suggestion, and Christ's Healing Miracles, ii, 151 f.

Tacitus, Annals of, ii, 37 ; iii, 4
Tertullian and Ecclesiastical Authority, iii, 20
  and Montanism, iii, 20 f.
Theotokos, ii, 155
Transubstantiation, iii, 124 f.
Trinity, the Doctrine of the, Ch. XI ; ii, 161–176
  St. Augustine's Argument for, iii, 6
  and Baptism of Jesus, iii, 3
  and Buddhism, i, 190
  Mention of, in Epistles, iii, 4
  Second Person of, incarnate in Christ, ii, 123
Two Worlds, the, Ch. I ; iv, 1–16

Virgin Birth, the, Ch. VIII ; ii, 113–128

Will of God and Prayer, Ch. IX ; i, 129–144
Worship, Protestant v. Catholic, Ch. IX ; iii, 129–144
  and Psychology, iii, 123

Zoroastrianism and Evil, i, 113.

For Product Safety Concerns and Information please contact our EU representative GPSR@taylorandfrancis.com
Taylor & Francis Verlag GmbH, Kaufingerstraße 24, 80331 München, Germany

www.ingramcontent.com/pod-product-compliance
Lightning Source LLC
Chambersburg PA
CBHW050634300426
44112CB00012B/1801